Five

Impossible Things

to Believe Before

Christmas

Matts intention us to prove th birth of Christ (Jesus) really was in every detail rooted in Prophecy.

The Star — Commentators think Matthew may be pin-pointing a Prophecy given by Balaam (Numbers 24 v 14) Although he was in th service of King Balak of MOAB — Israel's enemies — God forced him to bring prophecies to bless Israel & not curse them, under threat that disobedience would bring curses on Moab. However, in his own magical/mystic prowess he did curse Israel. Chinese records reveal a super-nova in 5/4 BC.

The Virgin conception. and old age conception

angels.

Text copyright © Kevin Scully 2009
The author asserts the moral right
to be identified as the author of this work

Published by
The Bible Reading Fellowship
15 The Chambers, Vineyard
Abingdon OX14 3FE
United Kingdom
Tel: +44 (0)1865 319700
Email: enquiries@brf.org.uk
Website: www.brf.org.uk

ISBN 978 1 84101 677 1

First published 2009
10 9 8 7 6 5 4 3 2 1 0

Acknowledgments
Unless otherwise stated, scripture quotations are taken from the New Revised Standard Version
of the Bible, Anglicised Edition, copyright © 1989, 1995 by the Division of Christian Education
of the National Council of the Churches of Christ in the United States of America, and are used
by permission. All rights reserved.
Scripture quotations taken from the Revised Standard Version of the Bible, copyright © 1946,
1952, 1971 by the Division of Christian Education of the National Council of the Churches of
Christ in the United States of America, are used by permission. All rights reserved.
Extracts from the Authorised Version of the Bible (The King James Bible), the rights in which
are vested in the Crown, are reproduced by permission of the Crown's Patentee, Cambridge
University Press.
Extracts from The Book of Common Prayer of 1662, the rights in which are vested in the
Crown in perpetuity within the United Kingdom, are reproduced by permission of Cambridge
University Press, Her Majesty's Printers.
The Collect for Epiphany from *Common Worship: Services and Prayers for the Church of England*
(Church House Publishing, 2000) is adapted from The Book of Common Prayer, the rights in
which are vested in the Crown, and is reproduced by permission of the publisher.
Extract from *Jesus Christ Superstar* used by kind permission of Sir Tim Rice.
Extract from 'Till tomorrow', from *Read On*, used by kind permission of John Dawson Read.
Extract from *More About Acting* by Peter Barkworth, used by kind permission of Jonathan Altaras
Associates.
Extract from *Human Traces* by Sebastian Faulks, used by kind permission of the author.
Extract from 'The Dogma is the Drama' by Dorothy L. Sayers, 1938, used by kind permission of
David Higham Associates.
Chorus from 'Anthem' by Leonard Cohen. Copyright © 1992 Leonard Cohen Stranger Music,
Inc. All rights reserved. Chorus used by permission.
'I only have eyes for you' words and music by Al Dubin and Harry Warren © 1934, reproduced
by permission of B. Feldman & Co Ltd, London W8 5SW.

A catalogue record for this book is available from the British Library

Printed in Singapore by Craft Print International Ltd

Five
Impossible Things
to Believe Before
Christmas

KEVIN SCULLY

Alice and the Queen

'Oh, don't go on like that!' cried the poor Queen, wringing her hands in despair. 'Consider what a great girl you are. Consider what a long way you've come to-day. Consider what o'clock it is. Consider anything, only don't cry!'

Alice could not help laughing at this, even in the midst of her tears. 'Can *you* keep from crying by considering things?' she asked.

'That's the way it's done,' the Queen said with great decision: 'nobody can do two things at once, you know. Let's consider your age to begin with—how old are you?'

'I'm seven and a half exactly.'

'You needn't say "exactually,"' the Queen remarked: 'I can believe it without that. Now I'll give you something to believe. I'm just one hundred and one, five months and a day.'

'I can't believe *that*!' said Alice.

'Can't you?' the Queen said in a pitying tone. 'Try again: draw a long breath, and shut your eyes.'

Alice laughed. 'There's no use trying,' she said: 'one *can't* believe impossible things.'

'I daresay you haven't had much practice,' said the Queen. 'When I was your age, I always did it for half-an-hour a day. Why, sometimes I've believed in as many as six impossible things before breakfast.'

FROM *THROUGH THE LOOKING GLASS* BY LEWIS CARROLL (1871)

Contents

Christmas: an impossible beginning

I have a friend who hates Christmas. It is probably because of an amalgam of experiences: the rampant commercialism, things that once went wrong in his life at that time of year, the general bonhomie which runs so counter to his inner Ebenezer Scrooge, even the fact that a number of times as an actor he has had to resort to donning padding, a red suit and a white beard to get some income. Whatever the reasons, it sticks in his craw.

He has a range of defences to deal with his dissatisfaction brought on by the season-to-be-jolly: alcohol, a heightened sense of frustration and dissonance with his fellow human beings, obsession with non-seasonal features, a black Santa's helper's hat emblazoned with 'Bah! Humbug!' but mostly the repeated expression of the opinion that it is all being done only because it is expected of us.

This was all fine until one year he found himself playing (and loving it) an Ugly Sister in a pantomime. As an adjunct to the fright make-up, the singing and dancing, the calls of 'It's behind you!' and the perennial banter of 'Oh, yes it is!' and 'Oh, no it's not!', he was required to do a party piece at a side function. It was then he found the perfect revenge.

He told a story he was given by a friend who knew his take on Yuletide. It is a presentation about how Santa Claus could not possibly exist. It draws on what some call a scientific view. It quotes physics and uses mathematics. It goes something like this: Santa has 31 hours to do his work among two billion children, of whom at least some are presumed to have been good in the preceding twelve months and therefore worthy of a visit. The gravitational factors of the world, combined with the speed needed to carry out the tasks on a vehicle weighed down by presents, towed by hitherto earthbound animals, culminate in a fireball of energy that leads to the destruction of sleigh, reindeer and the fat man himself. Conclusion? If Santa ever did try to deliver presents, he is dead now.

The story does its work well. It addresses the nonsense of believing in impossible things—and there is no shortage of them around Christmas. It is hard to know where to start. Just look at the number of people who take their children off on package holidays to Lapland to see snow, reindeer and the old man in red with a white beard.

Such enticements invite competition. There is even a company based in Kent that offers, according to a billboard on London Bridge station, a 'traditional visit to the mystical home of Father Christmas' as part of its experience for the whole family. (Attempts to do something similar in other parts of Britain were not so successful.) It claims to provide a four-hour child-centred event: it starts with a wax-sealed invitation from Santa himself; it includes an apprenticeship with the elves in the old man's toy factory, a hot lunch and a chance to assist in the decoration of a gingerbread house; you can see huskies and real reindeer; it culminates in a 'personal audience' with Father Christmas in his snowy woodland home. All this happens in the garden of England. This, we are assured on the company's website, will fill people with awe and wonder. One selling point is ethical tourism. Potential punters are informed that a family's carbon footprint in a car trip to Lapland in the United Kingdom is substantially less than that of a journey made by aeroplane.

I have another friend who, for reasons beyond my comprehension, packed a Santa suit into his luggage for a Christmas holiday in Cuba. He got dressed up in the suit and went down to the dining room for Christmas lunch in the hotel where he was staying. People, not surprisingly, reacted with surprise and amusement. He went from table to table asking if the people in the restaurant had been good. He made a particular fuss of any children in the room, who, it seemed, were most appreciative of the gesture. He later described it to me as 'one the best things I have ever done'! This may be an extreme case but people do indulge in some crazed activities beyond stocking up with more food and drink than is really necessary for one day's consumption. For instance, how many people—even good, Christian people—feed their children stories about Father Christmas coming down the chimney at night and delivering presents or indulge in the subterfuge of half-eaten carrots and mince pies? Even within my own family there was an expectation of reindeer excrement—though who was qualified to recognise it was beyond me—in the driveway outside the house.

The Church regularly tries to check some of this craziness. It speaks of the 'true meaning of Christmas' and then it plays host to a series of relatively respectable debaucheries: the terminally saccharine nativity plays by tea-towel-headed children and tinsel-lated angels, numerous carol services before the event, the seemingly ubiquitous mulled wine and mince pies. There is one church in the City of London that begins a round of carol services—sometimes up to three a day—in the last week of November. This is a well-intentioned result of double-minded thinking which tries to reach out to people with a gospel message while they are thinking about Christmas. Yet it is also arguably an admission of failure. It is an open acknowledgment of the infectious idea that Advent, rather than Christmas, is the season to celebrate. It also acknowledges the sad reality that by Christmas Day itself the world, unlike the Church, has moved on. Christians start when others seem to have finished—and they don't like it.

Advent was meant to be a time of sober reflection before the wonder of Christmas. It was a sort of Lent to balance the joy that is unleashed when the faithful gather to celebrate not only that God is good, but that the good and all-powerful God was prepared to become a helpless baby. The Almighty was prepared to become so at one with creation that he joined the ranks of humankind.

For many people it is hard to discern which is the more delusional: the midwinter festival of food, drink and fun or the claims of Christianity. They all have elements of what could be considered the impossible. This book seeks to unravel five impossible things that lead to Christmas. It does this by looking at elements of the pre-Christmas and Christmas stories in the Bible and it tries to relate them to the world we live in—a world too often looking for thrill and distraction.

This book is an attempt both to provide and to avoid diversions. It seeks to engage with much of what might be considered bizarre to people today: angels, upsetting the social apple cart, accepting life-changing interruptions, a link between heaven and earth, and our ability to recognise all of this. It may not convince anybody. But there is a possibility that it could lead us somewhere different, allowing us to look at Christmas, if not in a new way, at least in a slightly adjusted one.

~ Chapter One ~

The wings of an angel

In the pot pourri of literature we call the Bible, where history rubs shoulders with poetry, prophecy with genealogy, story with theology, there are many surprises. Anyone can point to a long list of seemingly impossible events. A personal favourite of mine involves a man, fleeing a task given him by no less a being than God, who hurts his foot when the animal on which he is riding scrapes him against a wall. Fury has no bounds, and the man starts beats his beast of burden.

Then the Lord opened the mouth of the donkey, and it said to Balaam, 'What have I done to you, that you have struck me these three times?' Balaam said to the donkey, 'Because you have made a fool of me! I wish I had a sword in my hand! I would kill you right now!' But the donkey said to Balaam, 'Am I not your donkey, which you have ridden all your life to this day? Have I been in the habit of treating you this way?' And he said, 'No.' (Numbers 22:28–30)

This exchange, not surprisingly, pulls Balaam up, but not in the way you would expect. The incident of Balaam and what many call his ass contains more than a modicum of the unbelievable. For a start, Balaam shows absolutely no surprise when the animal begins to talk. Shock or speechlessness would seem to be the appropriate response to this extraordinary occurrence. Yet Balaam simply proceeds to discuss the issue with the donkey. At the end of this interchange Balaam's eyes are opened to the cause of his mount's seeming disloyalty: 'Then the Lord opened the eyes of Balaam, and he saw the angel of the Lord standing in the road, with his drawn sword in his hand; and he bowed down, falling on his face' (v. 31).

The angel then explains to Balaam the reasons behind the donkey's actions. He tells Balaam how he intended to take Balaam's life, what he had done to achieve his intention and how the beast of burden had intervened to save him. The incident in Numbers has many bizarre elements, the two foremost being a talking donkey and an angel.

A donkey features in the surrounding mythology, rather than the biblical texts, of many of the stories involving the baby Jesus: Mary's journey to her cousin Elizabeth's house (Luke 1:31–45), the trip to Bethlehem for the census (Luke 2:1–4) and the flight into Egypt (Matthew 2:13–15). As the donkey is not actually mentioned in the Bible, we miss the opportunity to be amazed if and when the animal speaks. There remain, however, a number of incidents in which an angel figures.

Angels are enticing figures, which still have popular appeal. They are alternatively dismissed as impossibilities or heralded as the basis for some of the more weird and wonderful phenomena that parade under the title of 'spirituality'. A search of the Internet bookseller Amazon produces almost 193,000 titles. Not all of these, of course, pertain to the existence of extraterrestrial visitors. A more detailed search leads to the alluring, the allegorical and the laughable. In short, angels are interesting. They sell.

Why shouldn't they? They have so much to offer. One book puts forward the wonderful theory that violence—not global violence but personal, potentially harmful, incidents—can be avoided by establishing a four-way conversation. It goes something like this: you encounter a mugger who looks ready to biff you on the nose; you decide to speak to your guardian angel about the matter (angels, in case you did not know, are opposed to violence); your guardian angel has words with the mugger's guardian angel; the aforementioned aversion to violence results in the other angel counselling his charge against his intended assault. The end result is that you are spared a beating. Truly, I am not making this up. It comes from a reader's review that was posted for a book on Amazon.

When I was at school, we had on the wall of a classroom a large picture of two impossibly cute children playing in a field. They did not appear to be in too risky a situation: I seem to recall that they were almost gambolling in the near-perfect countryside. But the message was clear: their welfare was well and truly looked after. There was an angel, sculptured wings streaming in the background, reaching out his (it was definitely 'his') arms to protect the children from danger. There were a number of variations on this theme, one involving three children in a boat, another with a small boy and girl walking on stones across a brook overseen by an unmistakably female angel. In each of these variations the general well-being of the youngsters was not assured by their actions, whether reckless or foolhardy. They teetered on the edge of accident or disaster. Only the presence of the protective winged bodyguard let us know that all would be well.

There is something deeply appealing about having a personal angelic minder. It can provide a firm foundation for confidence. Confidence does, however, have to rest on a proper relationship between the one being overseen and the person looking out for his charge. I recall, as a boy, sitting in the same room where the picture oversaw the classroom, moving my buttocks to one side of my seat. A teacher asked me what I was doing. She seemed bemused and appreciative of my answer when I told her I was making room for my guardian angel so that he could sit down. I was concerned that mine and those of the other children, not to mention the staff's, seemed to be on the go and on their feet all the time. I wanted my angel, at least, to have a rest.

Other considerations about this classroom image came with time. The first was a matter of logic: if each of us had a guardian angel, why was there only one on duty in the picture with two or three children? The second was conceptual: how was it that angels always had such a recognisable form, one that was relatively consistent? It took some time to understand that this was a popular cipher with very little basis, especially in scripture.

The first mention of angels in the Bible provides more detail of their weaponry than their appearance. After the first man and woman in the garden had breached the order not to eat of the tree of knowledge of good and evil, 'the Lord... drove out the man; and at the east of the garden of Eden he placed the cherubim, and a sword flaming and turning to guard the way to the tree of life' (Genesis 3:23–24).

It is probably worth noting at this point that, for all the claims that angels are genderless, the Bible always uses the male pronoun when it refers to one of their number. We are also led to believe that recognising angels is not that difficult. In the first of many appearances revolving around the fertility of women who are believed to be barren, Manoah's wife tells him, 'A man of God came to me, and his appearance was that of an angel of God, most awe-inspiring; I did not ask him where he came from, and he did not tell me his name' (Judges 13:6).

Despite the lack of information, she seemed to have no trouble in recognising this being as an angel. Unfortunately, the passage provides readers with little to prepare themselves should an angel appear to them. Manoah's wife could identify him but she does not pass on any pointers.

A similar problem is swept aside by King Nebuchadnezzar, who was tricked into placing three young men, Shadrach, Meshach and Abednego, in a situation that was punishable by burning them to death. Despite the furnace being charged to seven times its normal heat, the king is amazed when he looks in: 'But I see four men unbound, walking in the middle of the fire, and they are not hurt; and the fourth has the appearance of a god' (Daniel 3:25). The king comes to recognise that he has made an error of identification and that the fourth figure is not a god. He goes on to declare confidently, 'Blessed be the God of Shadrach, Meshach, and Abednego, who has sent his angel and delivered his servants who trusted in him' (v. 28).

A similar scheme is hatched by those around King Darius, the presidents and wonderfully named satraps, aimed at catching out the three young men's associate, Daniel. Daniel is seen to pray in contravention of an ordinance and interdict which, according to the law of the Medes and the Persians, cannot be overturned. A breach of the rule that no one should pray to anything or anybody other than the king is to result in a mauling by lions. Daniel prays as normal, is seen and, as punishment, is put into the den of lions. He emerges unharmed and informs the king, 'My God sent his angel and shut the lions' mouths so that they would not hurt me, because I was found blameless before him; and also before you, O king, I have done no wrong' (6:22). It is worth noting that both royal personages exacted a bloody retribution on those who had accused Daniel and his three companions.

For all this, we are none the wiser as to how to recognise an angel. Although they are not named as such, one of the few descriptions of angels in the Bible is of the 'living creatures' that feature in the first chapter of Ezekiel.

This was their appearance: they were of human form. Each had four faces, and each of them had four wings. Their legs were straight, and the soles of their feet were like the sole of a calf's foot; and they sparkled like burnished bronze. Under their wings on their four sides they had human hands. And the four had their faces and their wings thus: their wings touched one another; each of them moved straight ahead, without turning as they moved. As for the appearance of their faces: the four had the face of a human being, the face of a lion on the right side, the face of an ox on the left side, and the face of an eagle; such were their faces. Their wings were spread out above; each creature had two wings, each of which touched the wing of another, while two covered their bodies. (Ezekiel 1:5–11)

It would be hard to argue this description of a 'human form' in an introduction to anatomy. It is, however, a key description inasmuch as wings are mentioned. It is odd, given that most angelic visitors in the Bible are recognisably human and are not physically described, that the wings have become the key visual code to their identification.

There are many extra-biblical reports of angels. They vary widely, in much the same way that descriptions of flying saucers or UFOs do. The outward form ultimately is secondary to a greater message: there is life beyond Earth and intelligence is not limited to humankind.

If we cannot find a ready guide to the appearance of angels, we need to look at what they do. Their tasks can be various, as we can read in scripture. Here are just some of the incidents in which they are involved:

- Implementing an edict or the wrath of God—for example, in preventing Adam and Eve from returning to the garden of Eden (Genesis 3:24).
- Leading the people of Israel from slavery (Exodus 14:19).
- Being armed with a sword to deal with the wayward Balaam (Numbers 22:23–31).
- Getting embroiled in heavenly battles (Revelation 12:7–9).
- Extending membership of the Church beyond recognisable practising Jewish people (Acts 10).
- Assisting in the escape or release from prison of a persecuted Christian (Acts 12:7–10).

Despite the range of their tasks, there is a consistency in their work. Biblical angels, very different from some of the bizarre mythology built up around their counterparts from other sources, have a direct link with God. More often than not, they are intermediaries, messengers of the Almighty. Supernatural they may be but, like all creatures, they have their being and reason in the Godhead. They do not exist in a realm of their own, a kind of parallel angelic universe. It is certainly this aspect—their being involved in actions through which God's purpose can be discerned—that makes them prominent in the New Testament stories leading up to the birth of Jesus.

The longest coherent narrative involving an angel in scripture is in the book of Tobit in the Apocrypha of the Old Testament. (The Apocrypha consists of texts that were not included in the official biblical canon by Protestant reformers.) The writing begins in the first person, with Tobit himself providing information: he regularly ventures to Jerusalem to offer sacrifice in the temple; he is generous in almsgiving to the poor, widowed and orphaned; he buries the dead after warfare (Tobit 1). Despite all this, he is the victim of catastrophe. Having buried the corpse of a murdered man and having chosen to sleep outdoors one night, bird droppings fall on to his eyes, with disastrous consequences: 'I went to physicians to be healed, but the more they treated me with ointments the more my vision was obscured by the white films, until I became completely blind' (2:10).

At the end of the third chapter there is a change. The story begins to be written in the third person. Tobias, the son of Tobit and his wife Anna, is commissioned to call in an investment made by Tobit some time before. Tobit gives a Polonius-like list of good advice (ch. 4) before telling his son to find someone reliable to help him achieve his offices (5:3).

It is at this point that the angel Raphael enters the story. The angel and Tobias, accompanied by a dog, set out. An extraordinary incident occurs by the River Tigris: a fish tries to swallow Tobias' foot. Raphael urges him to seize the fish, cut it up, set aside and keep some of its internal organs (which become important for plot purposes later) and then eat what is left (Tobit 6:2–5).

The angel brings a new element into the journey, reminding Tobias that his father has recommended that, in addition to recovering his money, he should seek a wife from among Tobit's kinsfolk. His suggestion is an intriguing one. Sarah, the daughter of Raguel, has suffered from an appalling run of bad luck. Seven men have been married to her but each has died before making it to the bridal bed (3:7–8). Tobias is understandably wary. He addresses Raphael by the name Azariah, who in turn advises the young man on how to use the efficacious organs of the fish. By placing the liver and heart in with the incense in the bridal chamber, pausing to praise God, Tobias achieves what none of Sarah's previous seven grooms had done: he does not die and goes on to bed with his new wife (ch. 8).

Raphael not only oversees the withdrawal of Tobit's deposit but, through the marriage of Sarah and Tobias, secures a substantial dowry: 'So Raguel promptly gave Tobias his wife Sarah, as well as half of all his property; male and female slaves, oxen and sheep, donkeys and camels, clothing, money and household goods' (10:10).

The successful conclusion of all these worldly affairs is, of course, a mark of God's blessing. A journey is made safely, a marriage is entered into, material prosperity is assured and physical health, in the form of sight, is restored (12:3). In recognition of Raphael/Azariah's role in all this, Tobit agrees with his son's suggestion that he should pay him, to the tune of half of what has been brought back from the trip. At this point Raphael gives spiritual and religious advice: praise God; let the world know of the blessings on them; pray with sincerity; give alms (12:6).

Then comes a stunning revelation. Raphael divulges that it was he who took the prayers of Tobit and Sarah to God. He was sent to test Tobit's righteousness to see if he would bury the dead. He was likewise sent to cure both Tobit's blindness and the curse of a demon on Sarah (vv. 11–14). An even greater surprise is in store for them when he tells them who he is: 'I am Raphael, one of the seven angels who stand ready and enter before the glory of the Lord' (v. 15).

After reassuring his hearers that they have no need to be afraid, repeating the advice to praise God, he says:

'Now get up from the ground, and acknowledge God. See, I am ascending to him who sent me. Write down all these things that have happened to you.' And he ascended. Then they stood up, and could see him no more. They kept blessing God and singing his praises, and they acknowledged God for these marvellous deeds of his, when an angel of God had appeared to them. (vv. 20–22)

The story of Tobit provides a key to the seeming impossibility of angels. It is not so much their appearance—Raphael does not stand out from the rest of humankind—as their deeds that matter. Yet it is not their actions alone that count. What gives those actions importance is their source. As Raphael tells Tobit and his son Tobias, 'As for me, when I was with you, I was not acting on my own will, but by the will of God' (12:18). Quite simply, angels on their own have no significance. God is behind the actions of angels. It is the power of God that they reveal, explain and channel when they bring messages and do great acts.

To a Christian this is of key importance. It gives weight to the appearance of angels in so many of the incidents leading up to the birth of Jesus. In three of them another angel foretells what many would argue to be impossible events. The angel in two of these incidents also bears a name, Gabriel. The first chapter of Luke contains a condensed narrative in which Gabriel appears to an old man and a young woman. Both question the heavenly messenger about the possibility of his prediction proving true: one is struck down, losing the power of speech; the other accepts her fate and erupts into a song of praise. The result of each encounter is a child, the birth of whom is a blessing to their parents and whose life ends in tragedy.

The first event occurs in rarefied surroundings—the sanctuary of the temple, a holy place where only priests are allowed to enter. As one priest, Zechariah, performs his task of offering incense on behalf of the people assembled for prayer in the outer courts of the building, an angel appears to the right of the altar. Luke tells us:

When Zechariah saw him, he was terrified; and fear overwhelmed him. But the angel said to him, 'Do not be afraid, Zechariah, for your prayer has been heard. Your wife Elizabeth will bear you a son, and you will name him John. You will have joy and gladness, and many will rejoice at his birth, for he will be great in the sight of the Lord. (1:12–15)

Instructions follow as to the rule of life the child is to observe, and predictions are made. He will be a forerunner; he will be possessed by the spirit and the power of the mighty prophet Elijah. His work will bring stunning results: wavering Israelites will return to their Lord; parents and children will be reconciled; the rebellious will be converted to the ways of the righteous (vv. 16–17).

In response to all this, Zechariah tells the angel what the reader already knows: he is an old man and his likewise aged wife has not been able to bear children. It is at this point that the identity and employment of the angel is revealed: 'The angel replied, "I am Gabriel. I stand in the presence of God, and I have been sent to speak to you and to bring you this good news"' (v. 19).

The same angel turns up in the Galilean town of Nazareth. Here he gives a peculiar greeting in which the young woman, Mary, is told that she is favoured by God. This bewilders her. Again, the angel offers reassurance and gives some startling news.

The angel said to her, 'Do not be afraid, Mary, for you have found favour with God. And now, you will conceive in your womb and bear a son, and you will name him Jesus. He will be great, and will be called the Son of the Most High, and the Lord God will give to him the throne of his ancestor David. He will reign over the house of Jacob for ever, and of his kingdom there will be no end.' (vv. 30–33)

Like her cousin Elizabeth's husband, Zechariah, Mary finds the news unbelievably startling. She asks a reasonable question: how can she conceive as she has never had sex with a man? The angel's response is markedly different from that meted out to Zechariah. Mary's lips are not sealed until she realises the truth of the message. Indeed, the angel's response to her question is straightforward and evasive at the same time.

The angel said to her, 'The Holy Spirit will come upon you, and the power of the Most High will overshadow you; therefore the child to be born will be holy; he will be called Son of God. And now, your relative Elizabeth in her old age has also conceived a son; and this is the sixth month for her who was said to be barren. For nothing will be impossible with God.' (vv. 35–37)

It could be argued that Mary's response to this message is nonsensical. An angel arrives, tells her she is going to have a baby without resorting to the normal human method, gives her news of her cousin's pregnancy—and she agrees to the whole package: 'Here am I, the servant of the Lord; let it be with me according to your word' (v. 38).

We will look at the radical implications of that statement in more detail in Chapter Three. Its consequences are similarly far from the norm. For many who read of Mary's ready acceptance of her fate and its outworking, the reaction is the same: 'It's impossible.' Sceptics' hackles rise when they learn that a young woman who could face terrible community retribution for her pregnancy might say 'yes'. The idea that her doing so would result in the virgin birth of Jesus is, to them, beyond belief. In the Christian heritage the angelic encounter is decisive. The course of history is changed by God's intervention in what the lyricist Tim Rice, in the title song of *Jesus Christ Superstar,* called 'a backward time and such a strange land'.

Luke's narrative has its own impetus. Yet common sense would suggest that the man involved with Mary—and Luke does not mention him until he is baldly named in chapter 2—may have a view on these events. His happy-ever-after contribution to this part of the story is, for many, questionable to say the least.

Joseph's reaction to the arrival of the angel is mentioned only in the Gospel of Matthew: he accepts the angel's command and takes Mary as his wife (1:24). It is worth noting, though, that an angel is involved, even if there is no name attached to the heavenly messenger in that Gospel. Joseph is a man of principle and, learning that his betrothed is pregnant, prefers to deal with the matter quietly rather than expose Mary to the demands of the law—death by stoning, as laid down in Deuteronomy 22:21.

But just when he had resolved to do this, an angel of the Lord appeared to him in a dream and said, 'Joseph, son of David, do not be afraid to take Mary as your wife, for the child conceived in her is from the Holy Spirit. She will bear a son, and you are to name him Jesus, for he will save his people from their sins.' All this took place to fulfil what had been spoken by the Lord through the prophet: 'Look, the virgin shall conceive and bear a son, and they shall name him Emmanuel', which means, 'God is with us.' When Joseph awoke from sleep, he did as the angel of the Lord commanded him; he took her as his wife, but had no marital relations with her until she had borne a son; and he named him Jesus. (Matthew 1:20–25)

Surprisingly, Joseph, unlike Zechariah and Mary, neither questions nor argues with the angel. That may be down to the different audiences Matthew and Luke had in mind when they wrote their Gospels or, on a much simpler note, it may be because the angelic apparition to Joseph was in a dream. Another such appearance later ensures the survival of Jesus (2:19–21), but that is to leap ahead somewhat.

The angel of the Lord in Luke returns after the birth of Jesus in Bethlehem, where Joseph had taken Mary to be enrolled as part of some kind of population count ordered by the emperor Caesar Augustus—variously termed, in different English translations, as the first registration (NRSV), census (TNIV) or taxing (KJV). Shepherds in the field are disturbed in their work by a heavenly messenger who pronounces a now identifiable greeting: 'Do not be afraid' (Luke 2:10). It is worth noting that no one in Luke's Gospel accepts these surprising events with the equanimity that Balaam displays when first a donkey and then an angel addresses him.

The shepherds are minding their own business when one angel tells them that an event foretold to other people has occurred. Just as we do not know why Zechariah and Mary have been chosen for their part in the story, neither do we learn why shepherds in general, or this lot in particular, have been selected. They are simply told that the Messiah has been born and are given the key to identifying him: 'This will be a sign for you: you will find a child wrapped in bands of cloth and lying in a manger' (v. 12).

Luke does not tell us if the shepherds are calmed by the news. We can be forgiven for thinking that they may have been further discomfited by what happened next: 'And suddenly there was with the angel a multitude of the heavenly host, praising God and saying, 'Glory to God in the highest heaven, and on earth peace among those whom he favours!' (vv. 13–14). This seems to do the trick, as the shepherds go off to Bethlehem and locate the baby wrapped in swaddling clothes, lying in a manger, just as the angel had predicted.

The apparitions to Zechariah, Mary, Joseph and the shepherds put a supernatural slant on a natural event, the birth of a child. The seemingly impossible becomes real; the extraordinary becomes 'normal'. It is, as the Christian faith teaches, a crossing of the demarcation line that many would insist exists between heaven and earth. As John puts it in the poetic prologue to the fourth Gospel, 'And the Word became flesh and lived among us, and we have seen his glory, the glory as of a father's only son, full of grace and truth' (1:14).

In comparison with these angelic interventions, much of the allure of angels today is paltry. Leaving aside possible objections that stem from the independent status of the manifestations—they act of their own accord—mentioned at the beginning of this chapter, popular culture seems at a loss when it comes to dealing with angels. Angels have appeared in many popular songs: they dine at the Ritz in 'A nightingale sang in Berkeley Square'; Tavares sing that heaven must be short of an angel because a particular person is so wonderful; Robbie Williams tells us that angels offer protection. These song writers want to express the importance of another individual to them. The person is so important that the writers make them otherworldly. Sadly, no one who has fallen in love can stay in that abstracted state for ever. The special person in your life remains special—at least, sometimes they do—but love demands a less rarefied relationship. Reality brings familiarity, and familiarity, if tempered by love, brings growth. These aspects of life, wondrous as they can be, are not so difficult to comprehend.

The angels of scripture, on the other hand, echo a great Christian truth: God's love has been poured out on creation. Despite the wayward nature of humankind, God has acted, sending messengers to reassure us that the link established at the beginning of everything continues. Indeed, God is prepared to risk the incredulity of right-thinking people by crossing the imagined barriers between heaven and earth and allowing the Almighty to become powerless. We will try to deal with that seeming impossibility in Chapter Four.

Questions

1. What 'impossible' events can you recall from the Bible? How have you sought to understand or explain them? Who or what has helped you in this?
2. How would you recognise an angel? Has anything happened in your life in which you believe a messenger has come from God? What happened?
3. Which part, if any, of the angels' involvement in the Christian story appeals most to you? Why?

Exercises

1. Find a picture of an angel that appeals to you. It could be from a Christmas card, a painting or an image from the Internet. If you are a member of a group, show it to other members. Tell them what aspects of it are interesting to you.
2. Make an angel. Let your imagination fly. What sort of things do you need? After you've made one, tell other people why you chose the materials you did and what they mean.

Prayer

O God,
in whose name messages are passed:
we thank you for those who speak to us
in the name of you—
the one who sends us
angels and humans.
We praise you for your embodied message,
Jesus Christ our Lord.
Amen

~ Chapter Two ~

Threats to society

'Trust me.' When put together, these would have to be two of the more alarming words in the English language. They should inspire a readiness to believe in the speaker, yet too often their utterance produces the contrary effect. You hear the words and no amount of sincere vocal inflection or facial gesture convinces you. What is it that hinders the readiness to place your trust in the person addressing you?

It may be that the expression 'Trust me' has been used too often by people who are perceived to have let others down. If someone has a history of failing other people, he or she should not be too surprised by a hesitant response to the declaration, 'You can rely on me.' This is not the sole preserve of individuals. It can also affect groups of people or even entire professions. Journalists and politicians face this conundrum daily: they realise that they are often held in low esteem, yet people rely on them to report events from dangerous places or to intervene or enact legislation on their behalf. The distance between what they say and how they act is the testing point—and this applies to us all, not only to those who work in the media or public life. For the Christian, the words of Jesus give an impetus for the assessment of others:

'You will know them by their fruits. Are grapes gathered from thorns, or figs from thistles? In the same way, every good tree bears good fruit, but the bad tree bears bad fruit. A good tree cannot bear bad fruit, nor can a bad tree bear good fruit. Every tree that does not bear good fruit is cut down and thrown into the fire. Thus you will know them by their fruits.' (Matthew 7:16–20)

The cynicism evoked by 'Trust me' is well embedded. It is enshrined in the top three big little lies: 'The cheque's in the post'; 'I can control my sexual urges'; 'I love you'. For all that, trust is a fundamental in human life. Children need to trust those who care for them. Indeed, they have no other option from the outset; they are in no position to assert an independence that is yet to form within them. Adults choose to place their trust in others. If they did not, no business could be contracted, no human relationship would survive and no communication of deep affection could be uttered. If we all responded with doubt to the invitation to trust another person, society would collapse.

We can see this in the Bible. Even the supposed pillars of our faith showed doubt. Sarah, the wife of Abraham, manages to subvert her chosen status as mother of the son of the covenant because, to her, some things are just beyond belief. One day, by the oaks of Mamre, Abraham runs to meet three men, who have mysteriously appeared near his tent, and invites them to rest under a tree while Sarah prepares bread and he arranges for the slaughter of a tender calf (Genesis 18). As the meal gets under way—and we must assume that no one was in a hurry, what with the killing, butchering, cooking and baking—the host engages his guests in conversation.

They said to him, 'Where is your wife Sarah?' And he said, 'There, in the tent.' Then one said, 'I will surely return to you in due season, and your wife Sarah shall have a son.' And Sarah was listening at the tent entrance behind him. Now Abraham and Sarah were old, advanced in age; it had ceased to be with Sarah after the manner of women. So Sarah laughed to herself, saying, 'After I have grown old, and my husband is old, shall I have pleasure?' The Lord said to Abraham, 'Why did Sarah laugh, and say, "Shall I indeed bear a child, now that I am old?" Is anything too wonderful for the Lord? At the set time I will return to you, in due season, and Sarah shall have a son.' But Sarah denied, saying, 'I did not laugh'; for she was afraid. He said, 'Oh yes, you did laugh.' (vv. 9–15)

Laughter is only one of many possible reactions to the seemingly impossible. The Bible shows many instances of people doubting, if not the power of the Almighty, the word of his messengers. In an incident involving the prophet Elisha, a Shunammite woman is quick to express her reservations about a prediction he has made. He has been the recipient of much hospitality from her, even to the point where the woman (no name is mentioned) has had a small chamber built on to the top of the family home to accommodate him on his travels. Elisha asks his servant Gehazi to suggest an appropriate method of expressing his gratitude:

Gehazi answered, 'Well, she has no son, and her husband is old.' He said, 'Call her.' When he had called her, she stood at the door. He said, 'At this season, in due time, you shall embrace a son.' She replied, 'No, my lord, O man of God; do not deceive your servant.' (2 Kings 4:14–16)

The writer wastes no time in teasing out the scene. He moves straight on to the ultimate response to the Shunammite woman's directly expressed cynicism: 'The woman conceived and bore a son at that season, in due time, as Elisha had declared to her' (v. 17).

This promise, fulfilled as it was, is succeeded by tragedy. When the child dies, the Shunammite woman goes to Elisha and rebukes him, saying that he had overruled her wishes in granting her a son (v. 28). Elisha calls on God to intervene on the woman's behalf and brings the dead boy back to life. It is peculiar that there is no report of the woman's response, given that her reactions have been so important in the narrative of blessing and pain.

There are many other Old Testament figures who fail to accept the seemingly ridiculous. Gideon is loath to believe that God has seen fit to set him up as a leader and warrior. After all, it disrupts his place, chosen or allotted, in the society in which he lives. Gideon refuses to countenance the prediction of an angel that he will lead his people to victory over their enemies. 'He responded, "But sir, how can I deliver Israel? My clan is the weakest in Manasseh, and I am the least in my family"' (Judges 6:15).

The angel responds to Gideon with a sign: fire springs out of rocks to consume meat and unleavened cakes (v. 21). Gideon's reaction is one of fear, followed by comprehension and fear: he thinks he will die (vv. 22–23). Despite these great and mighty wonders, however, he still doubts. He requires, and is given, more signs involving a fleece of wool and water. Gideon eventually goes on to win a mighty battle but only after God has instructed him to reduce the contingent of combatants he is to lead, to a number lesser than his opponents (7:4–8). By this stage Gideon appears to be beyond doubting his maker.

Communal as well as individual disbelief figures in a number of biblical accounts. The people of Israel, despite the astounding events of their liberation from slavery in Egypt through Moses' leadership, repeatedly cast doubt on the power of God. Indeed, Moses himself needs some convincing that he is fit for the task when he encounters the Almighty. He asks God who he should say has sent him as a leader to the Israelite people, and in that way he learns the holy name of God (Exodus 3:13–14). Even after this he needs more proofs and God gives him powers that can be used to convince others (4:1–9).

For all that, things do not run smoothly for Moses. Having been rescued from Egypt, the exiles question whether God can feed them in the desert (16:3). God responds by providing them with meat and manna. Then they suspect they will die of thirst (17:3). It is as though nothing will satisfy them. God's possible view on this repeated questioning of his care is captured by the psalmist in a warning to those who follow after:

Do not harden your hearts, as at Meribah,
as on the day at Massah in the wilderness,
when your ancestors tested me,
and put me to the proof, though they had seen my work.
For forty years I loathed that generation
and said, 'They are a people whose hearts go astray,
and they do not regard my ways.'
Therefore in my anger I swore,
'They shall not enter my rest.' (Psalm 95:8–11)

That section of the psalm would seem to suggest that even God runs out of patience with those who fail to trust him. The account in Numbers of God's response to the whingeing of the Israelites borders on the comic. The people reminisce about the good old days: fish for nothing, cucumbers, melons, leeks, onions and garlic were all part of their daily fare. Tired of the miraculous manna, they long for meat (Numbers 11:4–6). In verse 10, we read that God becomes angry, and he tells Moses to let the people know that they will get what they asked for:

Therefore the Lord will give you meat, and you shall eat. You shall eat not only one day, or two days, or five days, or ten days, or twenty days, but for a whole month—until it comes out of your nostrils and becomes loathsome to you—because you have rejected the Lord who is among you, and have wailed before him, saying, 'Why did we ever leave Egypt?' (vv. 18–20)

This is just the latest example of the Israelites' fickleness. While Moses had been on the mountain securing the covenant between God and his chosen people, they had turned to idol worship (Exodus 32:8).

Collective incredulity is a social phenomenon. Entire communities express disbelief when one of their number or a group within the community conspires to do something deceitful. This is manifested in response to offences from petty crime to organised robbery, and also when bad news is announced. The information that someone known to a group has died often results in the statement, 'I can't believe it.'

The theme of disbelief, as we have seen, runs deep through scripture: prophets cannot believe they are being asked to endorse the relatively weak and overlooked as potential leaders; the newly selected question their abilities; the to-be-led wonder why an individual has been selected from a certain tribe, family or community. Clearly God is disrupting the social order they have come to accept.

It should come as no surprise to Christians that this deep vein of scepticism is mined in the narratives that lead up to the birth of Jesus. Indeed, it is an important part of Christianity's very Jewish nature. Perhaps the most dramatic example is seen in what happens to Zechariah. His role is equivalent to that of Sarah, who doubted God's promise about a child. He does not have laughter in his armoury of reactions but he gets more than a rebuke for doubting what has been announced. The angel says to him, 'But now, because you did not believe my words, which will be fulfilled in their time, you will become mute, unable to speak, until the day these things occur' (Luke 1:20).

The consequences of this angelic threat are immediate. People waiting outside are worried when he does not emerge from his duties within the normal time. 'When he did come out, he could not speak to them, and they realised that he had seen a vision in the sanctuary. He kept motioning to them and remained unable to speak' (v. 22).

One fascinating aspect of Zechariah's affliction is that it provides the only instance where the use of sign language is reported in the Bible. There are many references to deafness (Zechariah is not deaf; he can hear what is said but is unable to speak in response) but there are no other examples of sign language being used.

The resolution of the issues of pronouncement and trust in this story is fully revealed when the son, the very one promised by the angel Gabriel, is brought to be circumcised. The people around Elizabeth want the baby to be called after his father. Elizabeth disagrees with them and insists that the child should be called John. Surprised, because no one in the family has that name, they refer to Zechariah, clearly expecting him to contradict his wife: 'Then they began motioning to his father to find out what name he wanted to give him. He asked for a writing-tablet and wrote, "His name is John." And all of them were amazed' (vv. 62–63).

They might well be amazed, because the naming of the child is but one of many socially disturbing elements in the life of John the Baptist. Indeed, the first mention of his precociousness comes when he is still in the womb. Mary, perhaps fleeing from a growing scandal in Nazareth over her pregnancy, comes to her likewise pregnant cousin's house. There the child in one womb alerts his mother to the importance of the other.

When Elizabeth heard Mary's greeting, the child leapt in her womb. And Elizabeth was filled with the Holy Spirit and exclaimed with a loud cry, 'Blessed are you among women, and blessed is the fruit of your womb. And why has this happened to me, that the mother of my Lord comes to me? For as soon as I heard the sound of your greeting, the child in my womb leapt for joy. And blessed is she who believed that there would be a fulfilment of what was spoken to her by the Lord.' (Luke 1:41–45)

There follows one of the great songs of the Church, the Magnificat, usually attributed to Mary. Some other ancient texts, however, read 'she said' rather than 'Mary said' (v. 46), which can lead to speculation that this revolutionary commentary on how God challenges the set order of society came from the mouth of the older woman. Interesting and perhaps controversial as that may be, the Magnificat provides an insight into the threats to established order that the acceptance of God's will can bring. A woman who is thought to be barren and beyond childbearing age is to be a mother; her young cousin is found to be pregnant without having had sex. Either of them is an appropriate spokeswoman for the power of God, who will do great things, show mercy to those who fear him for generations, display strength, scatter the proud, bring down the mighty, lift up the lowly, and fill the hungry with good things while sending the rich away empty (vv. 46–55).

There are remarkable parallels here with the Old Testament story of Hannah, who sang of the social implications when her personal life was similarly disturbed. Delivered of a son, after many years of having been considered unable to bear children, she praises God in glorification of a private victory. Like Mary (or Elizabeth), she foretells a subversion of the accepted social order: the bows of the mighty are broken, the feeble gird on strength, the full hire themselves out in order to be fed, the hungry grow fat, the poor become rich and the needy are raised to positions of prominence (1 Samuel 2:1–10).

The songs of these women are given another gloss when Zechariah's voice is restored after he has affirmed that his son will not be named after him. Whereas Mary/Elizabeth testifies and predicts more disruption in the world, Zechariah indicates a fulfilment of God's promises in his song, known as the Benedictus. Praising God, he points to a number of fulfilled prophecies: a saviour has been selected from the house of David, who will lead his people to deliverance from ancient enemies, something promised to Abraham and others. In the process sins will be forgiven and hope will be restored (Luke 1:68–79).

Those who go on to read about John the Baptist's later years might get a surprise. His life combines both the radical and fulfilling aspects of the Magnificat and Benedictus—a combination of achievement and subversion that is also a hallmark of the life of Jesus.

The Gospel of Mark begins with a quotation from the prophet Isaiah, a book full of the unnerving actions of God which are necessary to complete his work. Mark then alludes to the combination of fulfilled expectation and disruption that characterised the lives of John and Jesus: '[John] proclaimed, "The one who is more powerful than I is coming after me; I am not worthy to stoop down and untie the thong of his sandals. I have baptised you with water; but he will baptise you with the Holy Spirit"' (vv. 7–8).

If those words are not enough, what occurs next brings both John and Jesus and their dual natures together:

In those days Jesus came from Nazareth of Galilee and was baptised by John in the Jordan. And just as he was coming up out of the water, he saw the heavens torn apart and the Spirit descending like a dove on him. And a voice came from heaven, 'You are my Son, the Beloved; with you I am well pleased.' (vv. 9–11)

Nothing more is heard of John until the end of his life. Herod had taken his brother's wife as his own. John's criticism of this action led to his imprisonment and (in one of the more enticing narratives in the New Testament) his execution by having his head cut off and brought into a banquet to be presented to Herod's stepdaughter. The daughter had been prompted to request the execution by her mother, who felt aggrieved by John's public criticisms of Herod and herself (see Mark 6:17–28).

The nature of John's teaching was always potentially destructive of the social fabric of his time. In an early part of his ministry Pharisees and Sadducees join others who come to him in great numbers by the River Jordan to confess their sins and be baptised. Reminiscent of those who pay money to be on the sharp end of observational critiques from an abusive stand-up comedian, they hear a tirade delivered by John:

'You brood of vipers! Who warned you to flee from the wrath to come? Bear fruit worthy of repentance. Do not presume to say to yourselves, "We have Abraham as our ancestor"; for I tell you, God is able from these stones to raise up children to Abraham. Even now the axe is lying at the root of the trees; every tree therefore that does not bear good fruit is cut down and thrown into the fire.' (Matthew 3:7–10)

Later in the Gospel of Matthew, Jesus uses an identical phrase to address an extended attack on the scribes and Pharisees. Far from showing respect for these pillars of religion, he repeatedly rebukes them for a range of sins: not practising what they preach; wanting places of honour at banquets; laying burdens on people without equipping them to bear the load. After detailing much of what he considers their failures, he lets fly:

'You snakes, you brood of vipers! How can you escape being sentenced to hell? Therefore I send you prophets, sages, and scribes, some of whom you will kill and crucify, and some you will flog in your synagogues and pursue from town to town, so that upon you may come all the righteous blood shed on earth, from the blood of righteous Abel to the blood of Zechariah son of Barachiah, whom you murdered between the sanctuary and the altar. Truly I tell you, all this will come upon this generation.' (23:33–36)

The Christian religion is sometimes restricted, by both its adherents and its critics, to pious observances. That is not to suggest that prayer and worship should be considered ancillary to the profession of faith. Far from it—they are essential—but when faithful Christian living is confined to church services and prayers, its power is limited. Much of the teaching of Jesus is closed down if this is allowed to happen.

Christmas has, in many ways, been robbed of its potentially disturbing power. It is easier to drool sentimentally over images of cute babies in mangers, surrounded by cuddly animals, than to heed the disturbing call to make faith matter. It is unfortunate that many parts of the Church have become identified with 'niceness' and the trappings of power. Jesus often warned his followers of the pitfalls. Just reading his words above, addressed to the scribes and Pharisees, is sobering enough.

The tension between the fulfilment of expectations and the actual effects of his ministry can be seen in what Jesus had to say about the Law, the sign of the covenant between the Jewish people and God:

'Do not think that I have come to abolish the law or the prophets; I have come not to abolish but to fulfil. For truly I tell you, until heaven and earth pass away, not one letter, not one stroke of a letter, will pass from the law until all is accomplished.' (Matthew 5:17–18)

There is comfort here for those who want to preserve traditions; it seems to be a clear indication that the past will be honoured. This statement only appears in the Gospel of Matthew, however, and only five chapters later, with a parallel in Luke, Jesus is quoted as saying something that gives little comfort to those who emphasise 'Christian family values':

'Do not think that I have come to bring peace to the earth; I have not come to bring peace, but a sword. For I have come to set a man against his father, and a daughter against her mother, and a daughter-in-law against her mother-in-law; and one's foes will be members of one's own household.' (Matthew 10:34–36)

This disruptive pattern was a hallmark of the early Church. Peter has a dream that upsets him because it suggests that he should eat ritually unclean foods. As a result, though, he comes to see that the message of the gospel, while being of significance to the Jewish people, is not theirs exclusively (Acts 10:9–28). Peter then starts to spread the message among the Gentiles. When he is later challenged for doing so, he relates the dream to his fellow apostles and believers, telling them that he believes he has been told not to make distinctions between people. Realising that God's grace is universal, Peter's listeners are stunned into silence for a while but then 'they praised God, saying, "Then God has given even to the Gentiles the repentance that leads to life"' (11:18).

This amazing turnaround is perhaps at its most startling in the life of Paul, who changes from a persecutor of the church to one of its greatest advocates. His reversal of roles is initially both alarming and frightening to the community of faith but he later writes of how unnervingly liberating (and seemingly contradictory) the message of God in Jesus is:

As many of you as were baptised into Christ have clothed yourselves with Christ. There is no longer Jew or Greek, there is no longer slave or free, there is no longer male and female; for all of you are one in Christ Jesus. And if you belong to Christ, then you are Abraham's offspring, heirs according to the promise. (Galatians 3:27–29)

The Bible includes many instances of the subversive call of God. God repeatedly selects the seemingly weak for powerful roles, while much of the prevailing culture in the West today is based on celebrity and attainment—positively at odds with much of the Christian faith. Despite this contradiction, more and more 'megachurches', based on wealth and financial reward, spring up, often bringing personal enrichment for their founders. Their message is called the 'prosperity gospel'. Put simply, it says that God wants the best for people, not only in the spiritual parts of their lives but also in their material well-being. While this is true, the message risks being utterly corrupted by 'clever' preachers. They use the ruse of selecting random biblical texts to support their case. These include a corruption of the blessing promised to Abraham seen through New Testament spectacles: 'For you know the generous act of our Lord Jesus Christ, that though he was rich, yet for your sakes he became poor, so that by his poverty you might become rich' (2 Corinthians 8:9) and 'I came that they may have life, and have it abundantly' (John 10:10). I once listened open-mouthed and with increasing disbelief as a woman preached that she had to 'sow' by giving away a Ford before God would allow her to 'reap' a Mercedes Benz. Some churches claim that 'sowing a seed' in this way can only be done through their own organisation. Other churches (they say) do not have the blessing of God on their work, so supporting them will not produce any substantial material results.

It can be argued that this sort of teaching is a perversion of God's blessing, which turns the lowly into the powerful. It runs the risk of placing the benefits ahead of the grace of God. The Church has to guard against a spiritual arrogance reflected in material wealth: this always was and always will be the case. There is plenty of scripture to draw on here: Jesus speaks more about this aspect of community life than he does about sexual ethics (see Mark 10:23–25; Luke 12:15–21).

The early Church obviously had its problems. Reading sections of the epistles can make us realise how fractious and partisan its members could become. For example, James writes to question whether acts of favouritism glorify Jesus:

For if a person with gold rings and in fine clothes comes into your assembly, and if a poor person in dirty clothes also comes in, and if you take notice of the one wearing the fine clothes and say, 'Have a seat here, please,' while to the one who is poor you say, 'Stand there', or, 'Sit at my feet', have you made distinctions among yourselves and become judges with evil thoughts? Listen, my beloved brothers and sisters. Has not God chosen the poor in the world to be rich in faith and to be heirs of the kingdom that he has promised to those who love him? (James 2:2–5)

These words must send a chill down the back of anyone who has the task of meeting and greeting people as they come into church. They are likewise a powerful warning to 'busy' pastors who are confronted by difficult people in need at times when other tasks are jockeying for their consideration. It is not always easy to react in the correct way. That is why it is worth checking our responses to others from time to time. Have we developed a preference for some parts of our church community over others? It might be suggested that this is only natural. Indeed, it is, yet the Church should be a place where we question our 'natural' tendencies.

The lead-up to Christmas is a time when we read about interventions of God that turn commonly held truisms on their head: angels appear; an old woman becomes pregnant; a young woman conceives before she has had sex with a man; a 'wronged' man decides not to shame his betrothed when he learns of her pregnancy. The seemingly impossible is repeatedly the stuff of belief for a Christian.

These are events that rock the established social order. It is salutary for today's believer to ponder what is involved in the disturbing nature of God and the topsy-turvy world that a faithful response can bring. Elizabeth, Zechariah, Joseph and Mary find the normality of their social order shaken: God's intervention can be considered as a threat to their society. The way they react to that intervention has further perturbing consequences—one upset leads to another distortion of the predictable and socially acceptable—and the lives of their firstborn sons continue the pattern of unnerving other people.

The challenge for today's Christians is to see how that pattern plays out in their own lives. Does the gospel still pose a threat to our society or has it somehow been socially conditioned to curtail its radicalism? The answer to that question depends, in large part, on us. Do we take the faith we profess into the workplace? Can others see something in our behaviour that unsettles the norm? More worryingly, can anyone entering our assemblies detect these values in the way we worship and relate to one another?

There is always a flow-on from an event. No action is without consequences, although we might not be able to discern them immediately. This is something of a commonplace but has been arrestingly caught in poem and song. Ripples follow a stone being thrown into water, in the same way that the cycle of the seasons replaces one colour with another.

Jesus sometimes confounded the predictable expectations that we may rightly have. This is notable in his comments (known as the Beatitudes) to a crowd by the Sea of Galilee. In them, he lays out the upside-down world that he and his followers are to inhabit.

Blessed are the poor in spirit, for theirs is the kingdom of heaven.
Blessed are those who mourn, for they will be comforted.
Blessed are the meek, for they will inherit the earth.
Blessed are those who hunger and thirst for righteousness,
for they will be filled.
Blessed are the merciful, for they will receive mercy.
Blessed are the pure in heart, for they will see God.
Blessed are the peacemakers, for they will be called children of God.
Blessed are those who are persecuted for righteousness' sake, for theirs is
the kingdom of heaven.
Blessed are you when people revile you and persecute you and utter all
kinds of evil against you falsely on my account. Rejoice and be glad, for
your reward is great in heaven, for in the same way they persecuted the
prophets who were before you. (Matthew 5:3–12)

Questions

1. What or who inspires your trust? Why? How can you show someone you trust them?
2. How do you show your trust in God:
   - ❖ in worship?
   - ❖ in your relationships?
   - ❖ in your community?

3. Is there an incident in scripture, where someone fails to trust in God, that interests or troubles you? Is there a parallel in your own life?
4. Has there ever been a time when you felt as if your life had been turned upside down? What happened? How might God's presence—or distance—be discerned in the experience?

Exercises

1. Bring a song, film or section of the Bible that has challenged you or led you to change your behaviour. Listen to it, watch it or read it. This can be fun if you are in a group. Leave some silence to reflect on what you have heard or seen, then discuss your reactions.
2. Photocopy an image of yourself, where you live or your church. Draw on it the changes you would make if you could. Then ask yourself why you would make such changes. How might God have guided your decisions?

Prayer

O God,
whose ways can seem so mysterious;
give us faith
to trust in your ways
and be led into the astonishing power of your love,
in the present moment
and in eternity. Amen

~ *Chapter Three* ~

Daring to say 'yes'

One of the sad facts of life for religious people is that some of their number say and do some pretty stupid things. That is not necessarily bad in itself; it can be quite amusing. Sometimes it is rather endearing, as it focuses clearly on the flawed human nature of the faithful. After all, there is ample precedence in myriad sources for behaviour that falls short of the gold standard and the Bible provides plenty of examples. The apostle Peter is noteworthy for his slips of judgment on a number of occasions. One of the most peculiar occurs after the resurrection, when Peter realises that he and his companions have made a miraculous catch after a fruitless night's fishing because it is Jesus who has suggested putting out the nets again. Despite being stripped for work, Peter does a couple of things that seem to defy logic:

That disciple whom Jesus loved said to Peter, 'It is the Lord!' When Simon Peter heard that it was the Lord, he put on some clothes, for he was naked, and jumped into the lake. But the other disciples came in the boat, dragging the net full of fish, for they were not far from the land, only about a hundred yards off. (John 21:7–8)

It is just after this (probably the last in a series of puzzling things that Peter does in the Gospels) that he receives his commission to feed the 'lambs' and 'sheep' of Jesus (vv. 15–17). Then Peter is warned by Jesus that such a task will not be comfortable: 'Very truly, I tell you, when you were younger, you used to fasten your own belt and to go wherever you wished. But when you grow old, you will stretch out your hands, and someone else will fasten a belt around you and take you where you do not wish to go' (vv. 18–19).

More puzzling and bizarre than Peter's jumping into the sea, however, are some of the events that capture the imagination of otherwise seemingly sensible believers today. Parts of the media are quick to mock those Christians who get into trouble when they seek to live up to parts of the Bible: picking up snakes, swallowing poison and walking through burning coals, all in the belief that they will suffer no ill effects, or exercising distorted 'deliverance' ministries based on the command to drive out demons. Three of these, at least, relate to the commissioning of the disciples in the closing chapter of the Gospel of Mark (16:17–18).

There are other odd deeds carried out by those who claim to follow in the footsteps of Jesus, many of which have no discernible connection to scripture. An inordinate number seem to involve Mary, the mother of Jesus. For anyone seeking a range of mind-boggling peculiarities, often accompanied by the sort of passion that might elicit the term 'fanatical', Mary is without doubt a strong magnet. From a long list, one that tickles me is the 'appearance' of the Blessed Virgin Mary on a fence post in the beachside suburb of Coogee, Australia, in 2003. Hordes of people came to check out, gawp, venerate and pray in front of (or to) this wonderful claimed manifestation of the mother of God. Not surprisingly, there was no shortage of detractors. The *Sydney Morning Herald* walked the difficult path between reportage and satire, concluding its online account by quoting a local resident, Henrietta Dean: 'I see a fence post. And I have seen that same fence post for many years. If all these people want to come to Coogee then that's wonderful but the parking has become horrendous.'

There is also the entertaining account, reported by many news organisations in 2004, of a Florida woman who netted $28,000 from the sale on eBay of a ten-year-old toasted cheese sandwich, which had never gone mouldy and supposedly revealed an image of the Virgin. (My father-in-law, not long after this, sent me a plastic kitchen utensil that can create an indentation into a piece of bread, which, when toasted, could produce a similar outline.)

For readers of certain magazines and newspapers, Mary's image in a fence post is not that far-fetched. Their favoured publications dwell on the mind-boggling and toe-curling. I can recall one report (complete with hazy photograph) of the discovery of Elvis Presley's face in a cow pat. This was the same 'newspaper' that reported the sighting of a double-decker red London Bus on the surface of the moon. Another journalistic scoop came some weeks later when it noted that the bus had gone.

Some of the plethora of reported appearances of Mary—such as those in Fatima, Lourdes and Guadalupe—have had official approval from parts of the Church and have become centres of pilgrimage. This does not mean, however, that such places or sightings are universally recognised. Indeed, this 'official approval' is one of the barriers sometimes cited by those seeking a greater unity between different parts of the Church. There can be disagreement even within the same ecclesiastical grouping. The Norfolk village of Walsingham is host every year to thousands of pilgrims who are members of the Church of England, for what is affectionately known as The National. There are a number of religious observances, as well as a parade of a statue of Our Lady of Walsingham. In addition, the event brings a number of devoted protestors who usually take up positions near the market cross. They call out at the parading clergy and laity, often holding up placards condemning the 'popery' in front of them.

What makes Walsingham so attractive? The lure of the shrine today has its basis in a reported vision of an eleventh-century noblewoman, Richeldis de Faverches, who claimed that she saw the very building in which the angel Gabriel made his visit to Mary. In 1921 Hope Patten, the parish priest, seeing the popularity of the nearby 14th-century Slipper Chapel, which was in the care of Roman Catholics, about a mile from the Norfolk village, set about reviving Walsingham as a place of pilgrimage for Anglicans. He housed a new statue, first in the parish church and eventually in a building known as the Holy House.

A number of the many claims of visions, visitations and appearances of the Blessed Virgin Mary are controversial. Some are reportedly under investigation, such as the alleged appearance of

Mary—along with other visions of angels and Jesus himself—to four young girls in rural Spain between 1961 and 1965. It is a measure of the controversy that some, drawing on the consistent rejection of Bishops of Santander over the years, say the Vatican has rejected the matter out of hand. Others, ever hopeful, will say simply that the Church has not yet made a definitive pronouncement on the events there.

All this is the stuff of research, debate and, sometimes, ridicule. Depending on a person's view, there may be good reason to support or denigrate claims in these matters. Absorbing as that may be, however, it runs the risk of drawing our attention away from the arguably most difficult encounter involving Mary: the visit of an angel of God to tell her that she will break the normal rules of human conception. The visit has its climax in the events of Christmas: as promised, a child is born of God to a woman who has never had sex with a man.

A slight diversion may be required here: some people confuse the virgin birth with the Roman Catholic doctrine of the immaculate conception. This is a teaching, propounded in 1854 by Pope Pius IX, which claims that Mary achieved an exalted place in the life of humanity and the Church because she was the only person, other than her son Jesus, who was born without the stain of original sin.

Although the virgin birth is, for some, one of the most outrageous and unbelievable claims of the Christian faith, it comes with firm biblical foundations. Luke, with his particular concentration on the events leading up to the birth of Jesus, devotes especial attention to it. In his Gospel, the angel Gabriel appears to a young woman named Mary in Nazareth and perturbs her with his greeting, calling her 'highly favoured'. Seeking to reassure her, he tells her that she is to conceive in her womb and bear a son. Further, she is instructed that this child should be called Jesus and he will assume the throne of his ancestor David for ever (Luke 1:26–33).

Mary said to the angel, 'How can this be, since I am a virgin?' The angel said to her, 'The Holy Spirit will come upon you, and the power of the Most

High will overshadow you; therefore the child to be born will be holy; he will be called Son of God.' (vv. 34–35)

The angel goes on to tell her that her aged cousin Elizabeth, considered barren, has also fallen pregnant. It is what happens next, however, that is potentially perplexing. Having challenged the possibility of the angel's prediction, Mary does not go on to ask more questions or express reservations. On being told that nothing is impossible with God, her response is alarmingly direct: 'Here am I, the servant of the Lord; let it be with me according to your word' (v. 38).

Such a direct 'yes' to God's messenger has extraordinary consequences and, for many, it stretches the limits of plausibility. For people of faith, however, it encapsulates both trust in and response to God. It also needs to be understood in comparison and contrast with the earlier encounter of the angel with Zechariah.

Mary and Zechariah have different reactions to the appearance of the angel. Luke tells us that Zechariah 'was terrified; and fear overwhelmed him' (v. 12). Mary, on the other hand, responds in a seemingly more measured way. When Gabriel hails her, telling her that the Lord is with her, 'she was much perplexed by his words and pondered what sort of greeting this might be' (v. 29).

Zechariah reacts with disbelief to the angel's promise of a child whose future has been determined, and asks for a sign: 'How will I know that this is so? For I am an old man, and my wife is getting on in years' (v. 18). This is by no means an outrageous response in the circumstances but the proof, as we saw in Chapter One, comes at some cost to the priest. He loses the ability to speak until after the birth of his heralded son, when he confounds expectations by agreeing to give the boy a name that is different from all their relatives'.

Here is a first instruction in saying 'yes'. It is possible to agree to or accept something despite initially rejecting the suggestion put forward. It is, quite simply, acceptable to change your mind. In the case of Zechariah, he was not able to demonstrate his agreement until he was asked about the child's name. In writing down that he agreed with his wife Elizabeth's decision that the infant be given the name John, the angel's predictions were fulfilled. At this, Zechariah's tongue was loosened and he sang the praises of God.

Mary, on the other hand, does not suffer for her doubts. When she raises an understandable question—'How can this be, since I am a virgin?' (v. 34)—she is not struck dumb. She is simply given an explanation: the Holy Spirit will overshadow her and therefore the child within her will be holy and will be called the Son of God. The angel goes on to tell her what has happened to her cousin (she is apparently unaware of Elizabeth's pregnancy) and offers a rebuke to the cynic: 'For nothing will be impossible with God' (v. 37).

Mary's encounter with the angel (which the Church knows as the Annunciation) is the turning point in the history of faith. It is the locus where God's amazing grace takes over. Her acceptance is often known by the Latin word *fiat*, which means 'Let it be done'. Many people know Mary's response as it is used in a prayer called the Angelus, which takes its Latin name from the first words spoken, 'The angel', and uses the arguably archaic form, 'Let it be to me according to thy word.' The first three words of that answer have led some to speculate that Paul McCartney is referring to the mother of Jesus when he mentions 'Mother Mary' in the song 'Let it be'. Others, though, have suggested that Mother Mary was McCartney's own mother, who died when he was a teenager, or even the drug marijuana.

Mary's decision to say 'yes' is revolutionary. She allows God to do as the angel suggests, thereby setting in train a course of events that involves many other mind-blowing incidents throughout the life of her son Jesus: thousands are fed from small stocks of food; the sick are cured; the crippled walk; the dead are brought back to life; Jesus himself is killed and comes back to life.

It is for this reason that the Annunciation is important. It is a pivotal point of faith. It is where—not for the first time in the Bible—the natural order is turned on its head. It is, however, the only occasion in the history of the one God made known to the patriarchs when that God becomes a human being.

This encounter between a young woman and God's heavenly messenger is also the starting point for many problems that have arisen around Mary. For some people the seed represented by a virginal young woman saying 'yes' to God has grown into a forest of impossible proportions. The simplicity has become complex and, for some, a circus. Mention has already been made of the doctrine of the immaculate conception but there are many other accretions that have grown around Mary. Rather than remaining an example of an ordinary person lifted to an exalted position, just as others are in the history of God's ongoing relationship with humanity, Mary has become marked out in all sorts of extraordinary ways: ever-virgin, able to give birth without pain, sinless, taken bodily into heaven. Thus, argue her detractors, she comes to hold little of relevance to people today: she is so far above the rest of us that we can only look on in awe.

There is a possible counterbalance to this. It is possible to argue—and I do—that Mary's special place is actually defined by the child she bore. Her saying 'yes' allowed him to achieve full humanity and it was in that humanity that the fullness of God was revealed among us. So Mary is given a place of regard and devotion because she is drawn from the midst of her people. She is first ordinary and becomes, by God's grace, extraordinary.

Mary's ordinary status has huge biblical precedence. Many of the great figures in the Bible had feet of clay; even the greatest of the great were flawed—which is both reassuring and worrying. Adam did nothing to deserve creation. He, along with everything else, was brought into being from nothingness. He was the recipient, with Eve, of the gift of life. Abraham indulged in some dubious practices—not the least of which was giving his wife to other men—along the road to being the father of many peoples. Moses and Gideon, as we have seen, did not believe themselves capable of the tasks for which God had selected them. What is consistent in their stories, however, is the theme of blessing by the Almighty. It was God's blessing that conferred the honour on these characters. They were not, in themselves, worthy of God's favour.

There is a powerful follow-on from all this. The realisation that we might not be exemplary in our attitudes and behaviour allows us to see that we are not thereby necessarily excluded from the favours of God. There is a catch, however, which comes in the form of a question: how might we see ourselves as saying 'yes' to God today? What effects would that response have? Our responses might be life-changing but they are likely to be the result of relatively simple dilemmas. Should we begin the exciting and frightening journey of having a family? Can we make our weekly shopping reflect the concern we claim to have for other people's well-being? Can we prefer others to ourselves in the street, in our choices at work and in our community? There is a huge range of options open to us.

Is it possible that we can look to Mary as a role model in responding to God? A good starting point may be a consideration in some detail of what led up to Mary's affirmative response to the angel. We can do this by contemplating some of the artworks that have sought to portray the Annunciation over the centuries. It has been a very popular subject; for some artists, no doubt, it was a prescribed theme. After all, a struggling painter was hardly going to tell a wealthy patron (and the Church was, for some time, one of the wealthiest) that he wanted to paint something different. In any case, it has a lot going for it: a pretty young woman, an ethereal character in flight or just after touchdown, and the opportunity to paint a setting for the encounter—perhaps even a landscape seen through a window.

Studying each of the many elements in such a painting can be a hugely rewarding exercise. Identifying one symbol, such as a lily, and what it represents—in this case, purity—can add to our appreciation of the work of art. This is not the place to look at the range of symbols on offer, however. I would prefer to concentrate on the action—or, more precisely, the interrupted action—that is common to many paintings of the Annunciation. Chapter One looked at some of the postures adopted by the angel in this scene; common to many imagined portrayals of his arrival is that it disturbs the activity of the young woman, Mary.

It is in that interruption that so much can be learnt. Mary has been depicted as engaged in a range of tasks: reading (often a prayer book), writing, sewing, working in the kitchen, sweeping, weaving. Her life (even in portraits that place her in elevated, identifiably lavish European surroundings) is to be turned upside down. Whatever course of action she intended to follow has been disrupted and her current activity counts for nothing.

Two paintings and a sculpture from different periods give this revolution particular resonance. One is the Pre-Raphaelite painting, *Ecce Ancilla Domini* (the Latin rendering of 'Behold the handmaid of the Lord') by Dante Gabriel Rossetti (1828–82), which is part of the collection at the Tate Britain gallery in London. There are several unusual features to the painting. The author of the gallery's 2007 display caption suggests that the young Mary 'appears to be recoiling as if disturbed from sleep'. It is arguable that she has just woken up but there is no doubt that her posture is one of shock. This contrasts very strongly with many other, perhaps more classical, renderings of the scene. Rossetti's virgin is neither composed nor resigned; she is shocked.

Mary's possible distress at hearing the news is likewise captured by an American artist, Henry Ossawa Tanner (1859–1937). There are several startling elements to his *Annunciation*, held by the Philadelphia Museum of Art. The first is his depiction of the angel. Instead of a figure, with or without wings, the divine source of the messenger is rendered by a dazzling shaft of light. Mary looks to the source of the light, seemingly beyond the frame of the picture. Her hands are clasped in either prayer or anxiety: whichever the viewer chooses, it is far from resigned acceptance.

Both these paintings register the disturbing quality of being interrupted. Another image to do this is a metal piece by the British artist Victoria Rance in her *Annunciation Sculptures and Drawings*, which were displayed at St John's Church near London's Waterloo Station in 1997. At first the work appears to be a simple metal sculpture but prolonged viewing is rewarded. It is a tableau full of energy and surprise, just the elements we would expect when a person's life is about to take a new, unexpected course. There is a wonderful movement captured in what looks like the billowing of a curtain from a window into a room. There is power in the movement and strength in the pose, a pose that holds many of the traditional elements of the encounter. Behind, linking the would-be curtain to the window frame, can be seen the outline of wings. In this we can recognise God's messenger. His form is bending, like a knee to the floor, and we can trace another traditional motif in what looks like an arm pointing upward.

The figure of Mary on the other side of the sculpture matches the movement from the window. The outline of her shape can be read in a number of ways. First, she is turning away, almost fleeing as she realises the implications of the angel's message. It is as though the moment when the message is being delivered has been captured in metal. A less dramatic understanding could also be implied: Mary is looking at the angel but pulling away in horrified surprise. Whichever interpretation the viewer chooses—and the alternatives I have suggested are not the only options that can be read from this work of art—it captures very clearly the interruption of life.

Mary's 'I will' is anything but passive resignation to her fate. It is full of life and verve but it is also fraught with danger. Daring to say 'yes' thus becomes less like a pious acceptance of faith—though that is part of the religious quest and life—and more like a radical engagement, taking on the challenge of God's plan. That is what gives power to the Annunciation and properly ascribes to Mary a special place in the life and witness of the Church.

How many of us look at interruptions as unwelcome, knocking us off the proper course of our plans and ambitions, however laudable? If we are prepared to see the wobble in the wheel of our life as coming from God, we can move our life and mission far beyond predictable churchy concerns.

Parents and carers live with this unpredictability all the time. The needs of children, older people or those with some kind of disability can be immediate. Those who are called to care for these people have to exercise judgment to decide whether an intended course of action should be discarded in order to meet a deeper and more urgent need. Being open to disturbance goes against our nature, however. Many of us like to plan and see our programmes to fulfilment—even plans as simple as a trip to the shops. Disruption can therefore become a channel of God's will and grace; it takes its significance from our being prepared to put aside whatever we have planned in order to focus on different priorities.

That may seem too difficult an aspiration. Christians should see their role not in what they determine to do but rather in the way they meet the needs of others. The Christian's role is captured in the word 'service' and it can involve risk, even danger. As we saw at the beginning of this chapter, when Jesus commissioned Peter (John 21:15–19) he warned him of the cost of being a disciple. The warning came after Peter had affirmed three times his love of his master. He said 'yes' and Jesus then proceeded to explain the import of his acquiescence.

Any church that finds itself in the midst of many social ills is spoiled for choice in terms of opportunities for service. Being prepared to engage with those on the edge of society, who are probably off the church's radar, is risky. That way, though, Christian service can be redefined not so much in terms of discipling and nurture— important as these may be—but in terms of the unselfish assistance of others. Those others may not even recognise that the one offering help, the servant, is doing so for no consideration greater than the others' worth.

The parable of the good Samaritan is a helpful pointer here (Luke 10:30–37). Jesus mentions 'religious' people in this story only to point out the negative impacts of their actions. We do not learn what was on the mind or heart of the priest or the Levite and Jesus does not comment on their beliefs or religious fervour; all we see is the way they respond to the needy victim of a violent attack. The three passers-by—the priest, Levite and Samaritan—are all on journeys. Each has a purpose but only one is prepared to be interrupted, at a cost that cannot be reckoned on the spot. After carrying out some first aid, the Samaritan does more to ensure the welfare of the victim:

'Then he put him on his own animal, brought him to an inn, and took care of him. The next day he took out two denarii, gave them to the innkeeper, and said, "Take care of him; and when I come back, I will repay you whatever more you spend"' (vv. 34–35).

Directly after telling the story, Jesus asks his audience to identify the 'neighbour' of the man who fell into the hands of the robbers. Their response is immediate and correct: it is the one who showed him mercy. Jesus then gives them a commission: 'Go and do likewise' (v. 37).

The placement of this parable in Luke's Gospel is of interest. It comes not long after the commission and return of 'the seventy'. Jesus tells them to go with few worldly resources, 'no purse, no bag, no sandals' (10:4), and gives them a daunting job description: 'cure the sick who are there and say to them, "The kingdom of God has come near to you"' (v. 9).

The actions of the apostles and disciples often feature prominently in Luke's Gospel, yet here, and in the parable of the good Samaritan, Jesus tells his followers to carry out almost contradictory styles of service. One involves proclaiming the message of the kingdom of God after healing people, the other looking after others with no sense of reward other than the knowledge of taking seriously the command to 'Go and do likewise' (v. 37).

This should give Christians pause for thought. If we are open to interruptions—even those as seemingly incredible as happened to Mary—then there is a certain responsibility upon us to allow ourselves to be knocked off course. This means more than just allowing disturbances to occur. It may go against our nature, certainly as it is reflected in our personal and corporate plans. Individuals, groups and churches all like to dress up ambition in holy terms, yet God's disturbing influence might allow a greater way of saying 'yes' than we have planned for.

Questions

1. Has there been a time in your life when you have had a di[...]
   decision to make? What was it? What affected your even[...]
   choice?
2. Has there been a time when you felt God was asking you to agree
   to something? What was it? How did you discern God in the
   situation? What has happened since then?

Exercises

1. Locate an image or icon of the Annunciation. (You can download
   one from the Internet.) Look closely at the encounter between
   the angel and Mary. What do the gestures, body language and
   composition of the picture tell you?
2. Using the same image, just sit in silence in front of it for five
   minutes.

Prayer

Pour your grace into our hearts,
O Lord, we pray,
that as we have known the incarnation of your Son
through the message of an angel,
so, by his cross and passion,
we may come to share in the joys
of his resurrection.
We pray this through the same Jesus Christ.
Amen

n the universe

And the Word was made flesh, and dwelt among us.
JOHN 1:14 (KJV)

It is both entertaining and perverse that many churches, playing host at Christmas to large numbers of people for their sole annual visit to a place of worship, choose to read a passage of the Bible that is one of the most dense and difficult: the prologue to John's Gospel (John 1:1–14). The density and difficulty reside in the text itself—it is poetic, with multi-layered meaning—and in its attempted delivery. It challenges both the reader and those who hear it read. Here is a short extract, as an example:

He was in the world, and the world came into being through him; yet the world did not know him. He came to what was his own, and his own people did not accept him. But to all who received him, who believed in his name, he gave power to become children of God, who were born, not of blood or of the will of the flesh or of the will of man, but of God. (John 1:10–13)

The actor Peter Barkworth, who died in 2006, relates how he was asked to read the whole passage at a London church for the annual service of lessons and carols leading up to Christmas.

'Oh no, not that!' said one of my friends when I told him about it. 'That's the impossible one. Nobody ever understands it.'

'Consult a priest!' said another. 'Try and get him to explain it to you.'

Well, I didn't: I decided to try and work it out for myself. But there are problems...[1]

Of course, Barkworth is writing about its reputed impossibility from a performer's point of view. Any reader in church needs to be reminded that the proclamation of scripture is, if it is to be effective, a sort of performance. To that end we can learn a lot from those who earn their living by making heard the words written by others.

Anyone who has to rise to the challenge of reading John's prologue aloud could do a lot worse than to study Barkworth's approach detailed in his wonderfully practical book, *More About Acting*. The veteran actor offers good advice about how to choose which words to stress. It proceeds from an internal commentary on how to view what is being said. This leads to a series of decisions on the text, followed by methods and reminders on how to express those decisions. Barkworth concludes his thoughts thus: 'I found what I had to do after analysing it like that was try to throw the analysis away, and not exaggerate anything, so that the whole piece would flow in as relaxed and spontaneous a way as possible. This analysis remained, but only just.'[2]

This could be helpful advice for Christians in trying to express the wondrous impossibility of the doctrine of the incarnation—that almighty God became a helpless baby boy. The magnitude of this doctrine, which Christians believe and proclaim, is at risk of being diminished by the ever-present image of an imagined Bethlehem: the cutesy baby in the manger, often with his adoring parents nearby and a couple of fluffy farmyard friends for good measure. There is no harm in this image in itself: after all, Francis of Assisi, who is credited with the creation of the Christmas crib, believed it to be highly effective in telling the Jesus story and increasing awareness of the reality of Christ's birth. The tableau gave material substance to a story that was passed on orally or by being read. It allowed people to view the scene.

While seeking to capture both the ordinary and extraordinary nature of the birth in the stable, however, we risk being drawn away from the wonder and the staggering import of Emmanuel, God-with-us, to the saccharine and the too-easily-embraced. If that diminution occurs, all the danger is stripped out of the scene: the potentially awesome, even scary, aspects come later, in the adult life of this newborn babe.

To lose the danger from the nativity story is actually dangerous for our faith: it sells short the disruptive quality of the birth of Jesus. The nativity event has much to commend it: it has been presaged by heavenly messengers and apprehended by working people in the fields and, in time, it will be acknowledged by wise men from other parts of the world. Trying to capture all that in one tableau is quite an ask and, even if our efforts are laudable, it does not mean that the story will be universally accepted. There were those who refused to believe at the time of the birth and there are those for whom it seems impossible now. It should come as no surprise to the faithful that there is a deep sense of scepticism and cynicism in the minds of many people when this 'good news' is proclaimed.

One of the problems that the occasional or even the regular churchgoer encounters is a certain familiarity with scripture that does not draw on scholarship or knowledge. This is not to suggest that only academics can get the most out of the Bible. It is, however, worth noting that some background study can assist in our reading of the sacred Christian writings. Too often some parts of the Church seek to deny that, making claims about scripture that are contrary to common sense and tradition. Study can and should enhance our understanding of the Bible.

Each of the Gospels was written with a particular audience in mind. John's Gospel has its own agenda. After the poetic and elevated opening, it continues on a different course from the three accounts of Matthew, Mark and Luke. John portrays, not a different Jesus, but a Jesus who says and does many things that go unrecorded by the other evangelists. This Jesus makes long speeches, often with inversions built into them, and uses very few parables. Many of the events in the Gospel take place in or near the city of Jerusalem. John also makes it clear that Jesus is aware of the cosmic dimension to his life and ministry: he recognises that he is the Son of God, a claim that will set him on a collision course with the devout leaders and practitioners of the faith at the time.

All this is caught in the essence of John's prologue. Despite the

Christmastide associations of its opening 18 verses, the Gospel has no birth narrative: no angels, shepherds or wise men grace its pages. After the prologue, the writer moves on to John the Baptist, who encounters the adult Jesus with his disciples at the River Jordan and declares, 'Here is the Lamb of God who takes away the sin of the world!' (1:29).

Christmas is a festival that marks the beginning of the life of Christ and its festivities should undergird the significance of the event. The Church points to a radical revelation and revolution in the birth of Jesus. For many people it still tugs at the ropes of believability. For them it is potentially one of the most unbelievable of statements of all—that God became human—yet this is the premise from which flows so much of what gives Christianity its startling power. God, the source of all being, who is beyond all and in all, not only takes flesh but does so to the full.

That is a big pill for a sceptic to swallow. There are also many within the Church who struggle with aspects of faith and doctrine, as well as those who just do not comprehend or who misconstrue what they have been taught. I have a profound memory of an encounter with a woman who declared herself a good Catholic but flatly and repeatedly denied the possibility of Jesus being God. This clearly goes against the Church's credal claims but it caused the woman no trouble. She believed she had two relationships—one with God the Father and the other with the person of Jesus.

There are many fascinating views on God and how his interaction with the world in Jesus manifested changes. For the believer it is central that the events in Palestine over 2000 years ago have power now. That should hold true for people at any time in history.

In Sebastian Faulks' novel *Human Traces*, Thomas Midwinter, a doctor in the fledging field of psychiatry, gives himself over to rumination after a profound experience while looking at a 15th-century carved altarpiece in a German church.

Who were these primitive Galileans in their stiff robes? What had they to do with a church in Germany almost two thousand years later and with himself, living in the newest second of the present? They had doubtless imagined themselves to be the final word in humanity, as, at the moment they sat down to their supper, they were: like him, they rode the front edge of time into the darkness of the future. What he knew, and they could not have known, was that their species would change and that he, a modern man, would have developed in such a way that he was not human in quite the same way as they had been.

Looking at them, he saw beings in transition. One of them was endowed with a valued gift, which the others revered; but as he gazed at the muddled passions of the work of art, it seemed suddenly clear to Thomas what Christ's gift was. It was not that he was more developed or refined than the fishermen who were his Apostles; it was that he was less so. He alone possessed something their ancestors had lost: the power to hear voices and thus to commune with the unseen.

He looked again. What was so pathetic in the faces of Christ and of all the carved figures was their sense of absence. God was not there. Christ's eyes raked across the timber sky above Gethsemane, but he did not see Him. None of them had seen their god, and only one had heard him.

The physical absence of the god was the precondition of all religious faith. If the deity was there, self-evident, there would be no need for faith. But why was this the arrangement, thought Thomas; why should 'faith' be necessary? The obvious course for a thinking god would have been to make himself observable, not to make his power dependent on belief in the unverifiable. The hypothesis that underlay religion was merely an argument from necessity, because there was no need for faith unless there was absence. The interesting question, then, was whether that 'absence' was a caprice of an all-powerful deity or a real vacuum that followed a real presence: had someone or something actually vanished?[3]

These are the thoughts of a 19th-century doctor pushing back boundaries in a relatively new field of science but it is worth looking at some of the questions he raises about God. The first thing to note is that this passage ignores a central Christian understanding, that of God as Trinity. The Trinity points to three manifestations of the one God and includes the person of Jesus as his human expression. Jesus' ability to 'hear' God, as Thomas Midwinter puts it, would stem from the fact that he is that God. This is central to the Christian understanding of the triune Godhead.

The incarnation and the Trinity are both stuff for meditation and prayer. As the Athanasian Creed points out:

Such as the Father is, such is the Son: and such is the Holy Ghost.
The Father uncreate, the Son uncreate: and the Holy Ghost uncreate.
The Father incomprehensible, the Son incomprehensible:
and the Holy Ghost incomprehensible.
The Father eternal, the Son eternal: and the Holy Ghost eternal.
And yet they are not three eternals: but one eternal.
As also there are not three incomprehensibles, nor three uncreated:
but one uncreated, and one incomprehensible.[4]

It is not only the faithful who might encounter trouble with some of this, as the devout Christian and writer, Dorothy L. Sayers, pointed out in her essay, 'The Dogma is the Drama' (1938). The essay contains a parody of the traditional catechism form, satirising many popular misunderstandings of the Christian faith.

Question: What does the Church think of God the Father?
Answer: He is omnipotent and holy. He created the world and imposed on man conditions impossible of fulfilment. He is very angry if these are not carried out. He sometimes interferes by means of arbitrary judgment and miracles, distributed with a good deal of favouritism. He likes to be truckled to, and is always ready to pounce on anybody who trips up over a difficulty in the Law, or is having a bit of fun. He is rather like a dictator, only larger and more arbitrary.

Question: What does the Church think of God the Son?
Answer: He is in some way to be identified with Jesus of Nazareth. It was not his fault that the world was made like this and, unlike God the Father, he is friendly to man and did his best to reconcile man and God. He has a good deal of influence with God, and if you want anything done, it's best to apply to him.

Question: What does the Church think of the Holy Ghost?
Answer: I don't know exactly. He was never seen or heard of till Whit Sunday. There is a sin against him which damns you for ever, but nobody knows what it is.

Question: What is the doctrine of the Holy Trinity?
Answer: 'The Father incomprehensible, the Son incomprehensible, the Holy Ghost incomprehensible'—the whole thing incomprehensible. Something put in by theologians to make it more difficult. Nothing to do with daily life and reality.

Sayers' satirical conclusion is, of course, the opposite of what both the doctrine and faith entail. The Athanasian Creed, like the Nicene and Apostles' Creeds, also makes particular reference to the eternal life and mortality of Jesus:

For the right Faith is that we believe and confess:
that our Lord Jesus Christ, the Son of God, is God and Man;
God, of the Substance of the Father, begotten before the worlds:
and Man, of the Substance of his Mother, born in the world;
Perfect God, and Perfect Man:
of a reasonable soul and human flesh subsisting;
Equal to the Father, as touching his Godhead:
and inferior to the Father, as touching his Manhood.[5]

The Creed goes on to express this belief in more detail but the thrust of it is simple: the all-powerful, all-knowing God took human tissue in its fullness, by being carried in the womb of a woman and being born as a baby. Any mother will tell you that this is a painful and risky exercise for both woman and child and any parent will confirm the stark reality that an infant displays the complete opposite of the attributes many of us ascribe to almighty God. Babies cannot feed themselves; they cannot keep themselves clean; they rely on others to provide warmth. This is mind-boggling, yet what flows from it informs the faith. God was so totally at one with the human part of his creation that he became fully at one with it in Jesus.

Let me state it again—this has powerful implications. God is not remote from human experience, be it joy, pain, suffering or even death, because he has shared it fully in the person of Jesus. This gives an added layer to the words of Jesus, 'I came that they may have life, and have it to the full' (John 10:10, NIV). He gives out of a fullness in which he himself has been fully present.

In a dramatic sense, and one that points to the reconciling actions of Jesus on the cross at Calvary, there is an inherent brokenness through which wholeness is born. It is as though the birth of Jesus constitutes a crack in the universe: the separation of God and humanity is ended. By eliminating the division between God and creation, many of the earlier certitudes have been replaced. God is no longer distant; he is tangible. God is not invisible; people can see him. God is not beyond humankind; he is one of us.

This has profound consequences for the world. What Paul wrote to the church in Corinth about the death of Jesus can also apply to his birth: it is 'a stumbling-block to Jews and foolishness to Gentiles' (1 Corinthians 1:23).

How can we respond to what is arguably impossible? The starting point must be to concede that, for some, there is a real problem that goes beyond mere satire. It is unlikely that people who do not share a religious conviction will ever be able to win each other over by force of intellectual reasoning alone. Anyone who has done introductory studies in the philosophy of religion will have encountered processes that seem designed to exclude arguments from scripture or personal experience. Some believers find this disturbing but they need to remind themselves that embarking on such debate means entering into an agreement; if they cannot accept the starting point—the rules of a particular way of thinking—there is little prospect of movement on either side. Philosophy students would categorise this as a polarity of first principles. An imprecise parallel would be trying to play football with a tennis ball governed by the rules of chess: it is bound to end unhappily.

Having said that, what can the Christian offer to the searching sceptic? First, we need to be honest and concede the implausibility of using some of the rules drawn up by philosophy. We need to look to a neutral ground. I would like to suggest an approach drawing on the practice of another religion. Buddhism is classically a non-theistic religion. That is, it is not based on a belief in God. It has many manifestations and practices, with meditation taking a prime position in most forms. There are many variations in the style and practice of meditation. One form is to ponder the kōan . This is to take the seemingly absurd—the classic example being the consideration of 'the sound of one hand clapping'—and ponder its significance. Rational argument, discussion and debate are eschewed. The repeated silencing of the senses, to allow full exposure to the conundrum under consideration, is the aim. It is hoped (though it should not be expected) that sustained focused meditation on the kōan, which usually contains a paradox, can lead to a profound understanding of life. This is what Buddhists call enlightenment. A kōan, in many ways, seeks to defeat itself: it highlights the meaningless of the matter under consideration and, as such, can cast doubt on the answer.

Pondering the incarnation as a kōan can be a powerful aid to faith. In classic forms of Christian prayer, it becomes an act of detachment that can, ironically, lead to adoration. The person who approaches the mystery in this way does not insist on having an intellectual understanding but is potentially at the threshold of a profound spiritual encounter. (It needs to be stressed that someone who wants to conduct religious discussion in a set way—and many Christians themselves impose inherent restrictions on the way they will engage with the ideas of their faith—will not find this approach satisfactory.)

Acceptance of the apparently impossible is not confined to the realm of religious faith. Combinations of seemingly outrageous beliefs are not new. The appeal of urban myths (impossible stories that gain currency by repeated telling), conspiracy theories and the bizarre have a hold on many people's thoughts. I recall encountering a man after a baptism in church who told me he was convinced that humanity was the spawn of alien DNA. It was not an outlandish idea, he told me. After all, it was in a book. I congratulated him on his reading and asked, by way of challenge, if he believed everything he read. He looked at me quizzically and responded, 'But didn't you hear me? Don't you understand? It was in a book!' In addition, as a parish priest, it bemuses and confounds me that families who ask to have a clearly Christian funeral may, within weeks, be seeking the insights of a medium to discover how the deceased is getting on 'on the other side' and whether he or she has any advice to offer to those still living in the earthly realm.

Father Brown, G.K. Chesterton's diminutive priest-detective, points to the extraordinary readiness of some people to accept the bizarre in the short story, 'The Oracle of the Dog'. In it a young man relates the circumstances of a mysterious killing, in which the victim's body was found in a locked summer house. The murder weapon (the deceased had been stabbed) cannot be found. The young man is convinced that the only being who knows what really happened is his big black retriever called Nox. He bases this belief on the dog's behaviour: it stopped fetching walking sticks thrown into the sea and howled at what was believed to be the time of the man's death.

There are many blind alleys, as you would expect in a murder story. In the end, however, the behaviour of the dog becomes of prime importance. Father Brown stresses that the dog's owner, who has come to consult him, has confused canine behaviour with that of the Almighty. The priest points out that the dog yelped because a particular stick sank—and that stick had sheathed a sword, the weight of which took it beneath the water. The clerical detective concludes:

'The dog could almost have told you the story, if he could talk… All I complain of is that because he couldn't talk, you made up his story for him, and made him talk with the tongues of men and angels. It's part of something I've noticed more and more in the modern world, appearing in all sorts of newspaper rumours and conversational catchwords; something that's arbitrary without being authoritative. People readily swallow the untested claims of this, that, or the other. It's drowning all your old rationalism and scepticism, it's coming in like a sea; and the name of it *is superstition.' He stood up abruptly, his face heavy with a sort of frown, and went on talking almost as if he were alone. 'It's the first effect of not believing in God that you lose your common sense, and can't see things as they are. Anything that anybody talks about, and says there's a good deal in it, extends itself indefinitely like a vista in a nightmare. And a dog is an omen and a cat is a mystery and a pig is a mascot and a beetle is a scarab, calling up all the menagerie of polytheism from Egypt and old India; Dog Anubis and great green-eyed Pasht and all the holy howling Bulls of Bashan; reeling back to the bestial gods of the beginning, escaping into elephants and snakes and crocodiles; and all because you are frightened of four words: "He was made Man."'*[6]

Those four words, 'He was made Man', are the cornerstone of Christianity, constituting a new paradigm. When God takes the form of humanity in its fullness—from conception to death—the old order is consigned to history. This is the powerful message contained in the images we see on Christmas cards that portray the birth of Jesus in Bethlehem.

The faithful, while celebrating the events that occurred when there was no room at the inn, also look to the future of this child. Not only do they celebrate that the Almighty became human in humanity's fullness; they remember that he saw the experience through to the end. The Christian sees, in the life, death and resurrection of Jesus, a crack in the universe made permanently open and discernible. The events of the passion and Easter Sunday celebrate a turning point where death is overcome for ever. The singer and poet Leonard Cohen captures this idea in the chorus of his song, 'Anthem'.

Ring the bells that still can ring,
Forget your perfect offering.
There is a crack, a crack in everything.
That's how the light gets in.

Death entails birth; without the natal, the fatal is impossible. In that way, Easter celebrates the whole of life, not just a moment of resurrection. The transforming power of the events of Easter Day is a whole-life experience.

Christmas is a time for the celebration of birth and the birth narratives in Luke's Gospel capture this celebration in a concentrated form. The enormity of what is happening is brought together in the diverse nature of the people who come to recognise Jesus as the Messiah. Announced by angels, born in Bethlehem, adored by shepherds and later by the wise men, proclaimed by young and old, male and female, Jesus changes the way God engages with his creation.

There is an understandable reticence about this on the part of the central characters in the story. Amid all the fuss of the visitors to the newborn child, there is silence from those closest to the action: neither Mary nor Joseph say anything, and the infant—showing the complete at-one-ness of God in taking the human form—is, as any child is at birth, incapable of speech.

It is the subsequent events in the Gospels that reveal the power of Jesus. Trying to develop intellectual arguments to convince others of the importance of Christ's birth is perhaps an act of futility. How much more convincing would it be to remain, like Mary, silent but not unaware? 'But Mary treasured all these words and pondered them in her heart' (Luke 2:19). In this way we can let the extraordinary nature of the event percolate within us at a profound level. It can then radiate from our hearts to extend to the others we encounter. That is an exciting possibility.

Questions

1. Is there a part of the Bible that has sparked you to find out more? What did you do? What did you learn? How did it change your understanding of that piece of scripture?
2. Are there—or have there been—particular parts of the Bible with which you have had difficulties? What are they? What would you like to find out?

3. Which parts of the narratives of Jesus' birth of Jesus bring you comfort? Which aspects of them unsettle you?
4. Has there been a sign of light in a crack in your life? What was it? How did you come to discern the blessing in circumstances that originally felt far from blessed?

Exercises

1. If you are meeting in a group, ask your minister to respond to the issues that have arisen from Questions 1 and 2 above.
2. Find an image of the stable in Bethlehem. Find a place in the scene for yourself, imagining yourself as an extra, unportrayed presence. Sit with the scene for some time. Then offer the following prayer.

Prayer

All powerful God,
who became helpless in Bethlehem:
give strength to our weakness,
hope to our doubts,
repair to our brokenness
that we may become at one
as you are at one,
Creator, Redeemer and Sustainer.
Amen

Notes

1 Peter Barkworth, *More About Acting* (Secker & Warburg, 1984), p.

2 Barkworth, *More About Acting*, p. 29

3 Sebastian Faulks, *Human Traces* (Hutchinson, 2005), pp. 205–206.

4 The Creed of St Athanasius, The Book of Common Prayer 1662

5 Creed of St Athanasius, BCP

6 G.K. Chesterton, 'The Oracle of the Dog', from *The Incredulity of Father Brown* (Capuchin Classics, 2008). The story was first published in 1923.

Chapter Five ~

ding it off:
the star in the east

'We are all in the gutter, but some of us are looking at the stars.'

Most people who recognise the quotation above will probably know that it flowed from the pen of Oscar Wilde. It is spoken by Lord Darlington in the third act of Wilde's play, *Lady Windermere's Fan*, and has a rightly held place in many people's affections. The text was chosen out of a glittering array to appear on Maggi Hambling's compelling coffin-shaped sculpture to the author's memory, *A Conversation with Oscar Wilde*, which is situated in a busy thoroughfare just behind the church of St Martin-in-the-Fields in central London. The quotation holds the key to many truths, not the least being humanity's ability to delude itself: while our attention is elsewhere, arguments drawn from the discernible reality around us are easily avoided.

Stars themselves provide a good illustration of our tendency to be distracted in this way. Stars can become an unfamiliar sight for people who live in or near urban communities. The amount of artificial light being generated in and around cities makes it almost impossible for mere stellar bodies to compete. People who travel to more remote parts of the world often remark with wonder on how vivid and varied the night sky can be. Their normal circumstances are different: it is not that the stars are not there; they just cannot be seen in such profusion.

I have two personal memories of the awareness of stars in different hemispheres. On a trip to the outback of New South Wales in Australia,

I found the luminescent diversity of the sky truly breathtaking. The number and placement of stars were intense. Another time, as a pilgrim to the holy isthmus of Mount Athos, having awoken to the banging of wood and clanging of bells by monks whose task it was to raise the somnolent faithful for the first service of the day (just after three in the morning), I experienced a peculiar urge to reach up and touch the wonderful quilt of light that constituted the sky in that part of Greece.

The ability to see the stars—or not—can give rise to all sorts of diversions and perversions, extending to their very existence. Astral bodies that could not be seen were considered unnecessary because they were beyond human perception and, thereby, knowledge. Bertolt Brecht, in his play *The Life of Galileo*, presents a disturbingly credible scene in which the 17th-century scientist debates his discoveries of new heavenly bodies with a philosopher and mathematician who are speaking on behalf of the court of Florence. The institutional apparatchiks all refuse point-blank even to take a look through Galileo's telescope. They have other priorities that are more important to them. They will not look through the lens until they have established intellectually whether the planets are necessary to humanity's understanding of its place in the universe.

Despite the misgivings of the guardians of science in the Church, as portrayed by Brecht, people have turned to the stars consistently throughout history. Stars are involved in the grand and the minuscule; they provide material from the inspired to the bland. God, when he finally speaks after hearing the protracted opinions of Job, his companions and a number of other supernumeraries, challenges the one he has allowed Satan to tempt:

Can you bind the chains of the Pleiades,
or loose the cords of Orion?
Can you lead forth the Mazzaroth in their season,
or can you guide the Bear with its children?
Do you know the ordinances of the heavens?
Can you establish their rule on the earth?

Can you lift up your voice to the clouds,
so that a flood of waters may cover you?
Can you send forth lightnings, so that they may go
and say to you, 'Here we are'? (Job 38:31–35)

Songs from the popular to the obscure are littered with references to stars. Al Dubin allows the grandeur of creation to vanish because the singer is smitten with love (shades here of the Bible's Song of Songs) in 'I only have eyes for you':

Are the stars out tonight?
I don't know if it's cloudy or bright;
I only have eyes for you, dear.
The moon may be high
But I can't see a thing in the sky
'Cause I only have eyes for you.

Questions about the stars can bring more than a mere sentimental hook, as the singer-songwriter John Dawson Read showed in his song, 'Till tomorrow':

Fading light brings shades of night
Creeping to my room
And through my curtain I felt certain
I saw stars beyond the moon;
And as I lay there in my daze
I wondered, is it really true
That they're ten million years away?
Or could it be that all I see
Just isn't there at all?
It's just a memory, a used-to-be,
Of stars before they fall?
Or just a backdrop slung on skyhooks
To the greatest show of all
And we the players in the play?

This heartfelt intellectual meandering has also developed parallel paths in science and belief. Astronomers, like many in the scientific realm, are regularly updating and revising their knowledge. Advances in technology, computing and space travel provide new information that leads to new hypotheses and theories about the make-up of the universe. Planets are reclassified, moons are redesignated and stars are discovered. With this body of opinion on the distance and time travelled from the beginning of the cosmos comes more research and theorising, and so the cycle is re-formed and resumed.

Much of this passes the ordinary person by. The competing workings of scientists are rightly the preserve of academe. The needs of astronomers impact on the journalistically-led concerns of the masses only when there is a potentially controversial demand for funding to extend the exploration of space. To prepare, equip and support a probe into the ether inevitably involves pound and dollar signs. Relative moral arguments come to the fore: how can the huge expense on an exploratory mission to relatively unknown parts of the universe, which will take years to reach its destination with no guarantee of success, be justified when parts of humanity still live in dire poverty without the basics of clean water and sanitation? The questions are not new and the competing responses to them are never conclusive.

Another area of consistent and concentrated interest in the stars is more dubious. Even otherwise respected newspapers carry columns devoted to one person's interpretation of the events of individual lives based on the movement of planets and stars. The zodiac has a long and varied history. Symbols of heavenly bodies feature in many ancient, historic and religious buildings, as reminders of humanity's humble place in a wider order. The newspaper horoscopes, however, can overturn this sense of humility, manifesting a branch of knowledge that has a more questionable reliability and terminates in self-absorption. The Archbishop of Canterbury, Rowan Williams, once began a lecture to a conference in Cambridge with two simple questions and responses: 'What is the function of the world? To give glory to God. What is the function of the Church? To remind the world of its purpose.' As the psalmist writes, 'The heavens are telling the glory of God; and the firmament proclaims his handiwork (Psalm 19:1). This is a far cry from what many look to the skies for. Their view is that the heavens exist to explain an individual's place in the world. There is a fundamental clash of values in that confrontation.

Doubts over the efficacy of using the stars for such ends are raised in the Apocrypha:

For all people who were ignorant of God were foolish by nature;
and they were unable from the good things that are seen
to know the one who exists,
nor did they recognise the artisan while paying heed to his works;
but they supposed that either fire or wind or swift air,
or the circle of the stars, or turbulent water,
or the luminaries of heaven were the gods that rule the world.
If through delight in the beauty of these things
people assumed them to be gods,
let them know how much better than these is their Lord,
for the author of beauty created them. (Wisdom of Solomon 13:1–3)

My own avowed cynicism about the use of the stars to interpret personality and events was well tested when I worked in the theatre, whose practitioners appeared to have a disproportionate interest in and susceptibility to the weird, wacky and wonderful. A fellow actor was once holding forth on the fate-like influence on her life of the movement of heavenly bodies. I responded with a well-rehearsed retort: how can an entire group of people, who have nothing in common but a date of birth, be categorised with the same personality and predicted life events? The woman looked momentarily pained before asking me my birth date. She sighed, looked to the ceiling and informed me that my scepticism was only to be expected from a 'typical Sagittarius'.

Astrology has its significance elevated by the Greek root of the latter part of the word. *Logos* means 'word' (which carries particularly power for Christians: see John 1), and its extension into terms ending in '-ology' usually indicates science or knowledge of one particular field. Astronomy, on the other hand, is downgraded by its Greek root, as *nemo* means 'arrange'. So 'astrology' seems to suggest skill and research, while 'astronomy' is relegated to mere observation—the 'arrangement of stars'. Neither word adequately describes what its study entails.

It would be wrong for people of faith to take a too high-handed attitude in this area. Scripture's accounts of the beginnings of the extra-terrestrial world are hardly the stuff of solid scientific knowledge. Those who advocate intelligent design or 'creation science' are only the latest arrivals in a series of people who make arguably untenable claims about the Christian holy book. The Church has a chequered history in this field. Galileo Galilei was condemned as a heretic for pushing back the boundaries of knowledge and challenging the existing view that the planets revolved around the earth. He pointed the way to a complex and more beautiful vision of interconnecting heavenly bodies. The earth, while special, was only one such body in a vast order.

In Brecht's play, *The Life of Galileo*, this claim leads to a dramatic collision of the forces of power and knowledge. In one scene, the scientist speaks passionately with a couple of cardinals about how knowledge can change. He uses a personal recollection of being on a ship as a child: he cried out when he saw the shore apparently moving away from the boat. His adult understanding, of course, informed him that he had been mistaken: what actually occurred was that the craft moved away from the shore. This is his riposte to one of the prelates, who quotes Ecclesiastes 1:5: 'The sun rises and the sun goes down, and hurries to the place where it rises.' The event itself does not change; what may change is the way we understand it—as we realise on rereading the Genesis creation accounts.

And God said, 'Let there be lights in the dome of the sky to separate the day from the night; and let them be for signs and for seasons and for days and years, and let them be lights in the dome of the sky to light upon the earth.' And it was so. God made the two great lights—the greater light to rule the day and the lesser light to rule the night—and the stars. God set them in the dome of the sky to give light upon the earth, to rule over the day and over the night, and to separate the light from darkness. And God saw that it was good. And there was evening and there was morning, the fourth day. (Genesis 1:14–19)

This comes after an account of the creation of light, which divides night from day (vv. 3–4), the waters being held above the earth by a dome (vv. 6–9) and vegetation being provided (vv. 11–12). It is puzzling that creationists purport to find solid substance for their beliefs in these biblical texts.

The Bible does, however, describe many startling events in the sky. Even without the appearance of stars, the skies remain potent indicators of the Almighty's relationship with his chosen people. The safe passage of the Israelites from slavery to the verge of the promised land, under the leadership of Moses, is guided by God through signs in the sky.

The Lord went in front of them in a pillar of cloud by day, to lead them along the way, and in a pillar of fire by night, to give them light, so that they might travel by day and by night. Neither the pillar of cloud by day nor the pillar of fire by night left its place in front of the people. (Exodus 13:21–22)

At the very time when God lays down his covenant, along with the details of the response the Israelites are commanded to make, the sky appears to cover the mountain (Exodus 19:16–20). It is a dramatic scene, reminiscent of an earlier celestial assurance—when God spoke to Noah after the cataclysmic events of the flood.

God said, 'This is the sign of the covenant that I make between me and you and every living creature that is with you, for all future generations: I have set my bow in the clouds, and it shall be a sign of the covenant between me and the earth. When I bring clouds over the earth and the bow is seen in the clouds, I will remember my covenant that is between me and you and every living creature of all flesh; and the waters shall never again become a flood to destroy all flesh. When the bow is in the clouds, I will see it and remember the everlasting covenant between God and every living creature of all flesh that is on the earth.' (Genesis 9:12–16)

The most startling feature of this account is that, even though God himself sets in place the events that lead to the rainbow, they will remind God of the covenant. It is assumed that humankind will also recall the covenant when they see the same sign.

Christmas is the time when we can see that covenant renewed and altered—a season when, instead of looking to the sky, we look to one of our own. The rainbow becomes a person and the assurance of God's love is moved from the heavenly to the earthly. It is a quintessentially human event, albeit one replete with the power of almighty God.

One of the most significant events in the Christmas story depends on a star in the sky. It can seem odd to someone reading Matthew's Gospel that only the wise men from the east notice the celestial pointers to the significance of what has occurred in Bethlehem. It is the arguably Gnostic understanding of their observations that leads some commentators to suggest that the magi were astrologers: they have recognised a portent in the skies that has reached fulfilment, and they are on a journey to record its significance. They move from being observers to explorers with a purpose, like those who set out to locate the source of a great, flowing river. Yet the wise men also have a larger purpose; they want to do more than find where Jesus is, as can be seen in their question and explanation to King Herod: 'Where is the child who has been born king of the Jews? For we observed his star at its rising, and have come to pay him homage' (Matthew 2:2).

Herod's reaction is one of perturbation. His social order, and especially his dominant place within it, has been overturned by the birth of this new regent. The ultimate threat to civil society has been manifested: the king believes that he has been deposed. The concentrated interchange that follows confirms this belief. Herod calls on the religious leaders and scholars of the day to provide the information he seeks: where is this usurper to be found? Despite being told that the event will have taken place in Bethlehem (v. 5),

Herod wants more precise information. He desires an exact location: 'Then he sent them to Bethlehem, saying, "Go and search diligently for the child; and when you have found him, bring me word so that I may also go and pay homage"' (v. 8).

Once again, the star seems to provide private information to the travellers from afar: 'and there, ahead of them, went the star that they had seen at its rising, until it stopped over the place where the child was' (v. 9). What follows is the culmination of what some would argue is impossible. The wise men are the only ones to have seen the star and recognised its significance. Then, having been prepared for what they encounter, they present symbolic gifts. They already know what they need to do when they find the one for whom they are searching. This is no random excursion but one of recognition and proclamation. Their actions in presenting the gifts are made explicit by J.H. Hopkins in the much-loved and instructive Epiphany carol, 'We three kings from Orient are'. The number of 'kings' matches the number of gifts they bring: gold to acknowledge a king in the earthly realm; frankincense to indicate the godly nature of the child; the bitter perfume of myrrh to alert the observer that the joyfulness of the birth will have a mortal end.

Those elements represent barriers to believability for some people. How can the all-powerful God be reduced to a baby who cannot feed, clothe, warm or even clean himself? How can the eternal be found in one so clearly identifiable as a human being and thereby be doomed to mortality? How can a king be one whose circumstances at birth are as far from a royal hall as can be imagined?

It is worth reminding ourselves that the feast of the Epiphany comes later, despite the presence of the kings, who also collected the extra-scriptural names of Caspar, Melchior and Balthassar, as fixtures in so many nativity plays. Yet scripture supports a longer period of time than the customary twelve days that the Church uses to separate Christmas from Epiphany. It is generally thought that, by the time the magi appear, the holy family must have moved well beyond the incommodious accommodation forced upon them when they first arrived in Bethlehem. Some scholars suggest that up to two years had passed, based on the age of the children killed by Herod's troops after he has realised that the magi are not going to provide more information on the whereabouts of the newly-born monarch:

Then Herod, when he saw that he had been tricked by the wise men, was in a furious rage, and he sent and killed all the male children in Bethlehem and in all that region who were two years old or under, according to the time which he had ascertained from the wise men. (Matthew 2:16, RSV)

Before this horrifying act, Matthew describes the arrival of the wise men at their destination: 'On entering the house, they saw the child with Mary his mother; and they knelt down and paid him homage' (2:11). The mention of a house adds evidence to the suggestion that time has passed.

This scene rounds off the narrative in a pleasing manner—but it could be more startling, according to a shop I found on a recent visit to Venice. It was selling a wide range of Christmas crib adornments: the ubiquitous Italian water feature, the various tradespeople at work at oven, forge or factory, and the children selling their wares. There was one scene, however, that truly made me do a double take: baby Jesus lay in his crib, overseen by a looming Father Christmas paying homage in much the same way as the wise men.

The star is one of the final flourishes in the Gospel narratives of Jesus' birth, pointing beyond the limited and limiting beliefs of many people. In Luke's Gospel, the relatively poor, simple, uneducated and earthbound folk are typified by the shepherds. They are counterbalanced by the angels in the sky and the skyward-looking wise men. Here the skies hold both natural and supernatural bodies that acknowledge the birth of the hope of Israel. Luke's narrative also contains a balance of acclamation: the unborn John the Baptist welcomes a fellow new life, while the old, represented by Anna and Simeon, are united in rejoicing that the Christ has been manifested; both men and women celebrate, in the persons of Zechariah and Elizabeth. This coming together of seeming opposites is one of the most compelling elements of the Christian story.

The delay in the arrival of the wise men has further significance, though. It points not only to a long journey but also to many different ways of spreading the information. This should come as no surprise to those involved in spreading the good news of Jesus. Even in these days of instant communication around the globe, there are still many people who have not heard the stories about Jesus of Nazareth, let alone understood the importance Christians place on them. The journey of the magi can be seen as a metaphor for this: it takes time for the message to get abroad, just as it can take time for people to realise its significance for them. We can interpret this as a caution against the expectation of dynamic, universal conversion. God's way is more gradual. The passing on of news and the recognition of its importance may not be as cataclysmic or sudden as some may hope but it remains possible that the gospel can be spread throughout the world and down through the generations. The magi's journey is a metaphor of activity, not one of resigned acceptance.

The universalism of Christianity should be the impetus for believers to pass on the message. There always have been and always will be arguments over how this should be done, yet we can agree that we have good news to spread. That is why the inclination of some parts of the Church to associate solely with their own self-approved associates is regrettable. It acts against the spirit of wonder and delight encapsulated in the Gospels. The early Church certainly recognised this tendency. As Peter said in the house of Cornelius in Caesarea, 'I truly understand that God shows no partiality, but in every nation anyone who fears him and does what is right is acceptable to him. You know the message he sent to the people of Israel, preaching peace by Jesus Christ—he is Lord of all' (Acts 10:34–36).

This echoes the wonderful words of Paul to the church in Galatia:

For in Christ Jesus you are all children of God through faith. As many of you were baptised into Christ have clothed yourselves with Christ. There is no longer Jew or Greek, there is no longer slave or free, there is no longer male and female; for all of you are one in Christ Jesus. (Galatians 3:26–28)

Such a disruptive agenda is not appealing to everyone. It is often easier to keep to our preconceived ideas. There are times, however, when we can cross borders in our thinking. As a writer, I explored these ideas in a stage play, *Hard Up*, which was seen at the Griffin Theatre in Sydney, Australia, in 1993. The play is set in a miserable part of that city's outer fringes, most of the characters being users of a rundown and besieged community centre. For all that, a gaze into the night sky leads one of the characters to wonder if there is a beneficent force looking down on the world. It is perhaps easy solace to offer but this is an echo of Rowan Williams' two-pronged question and answer: the Church's job is to remind the world of its purpose.

This universal imperative can be uncomfortable: it is easier to seek the company of fellow travellers. However, perhaps the most difficult element to accept is that Christians should be challenging both sectionalism and arrogance. As hymn writer Edward Burns declares, 'Jesus is Lord of all the earth.' We can look to the skies to challenge us. We can remind ourselves, if we live in urban areas, that we may not be able to see the stars but that does not mean they are no longer there. We do not have to confine ourselves to Lord Darlington's gutter. We can understand that our world has provided one kind of illumination to counter another, more ancient form of light. Unlike Galileo, we have to rely on knowledge that is not immediately discernible to the naked eye, but this is far from relegating our beliefs to the realm of superstition. We can rely on accrued information from more than mere individual experience, giving us a collective strength.

That is of prime importance to the Christian, and is summarised in Edward Burns' hymn, mentioned above:

We have a gospel to proclaim,
Good news for men in all the earth.
The gospel of a Saviour's name:
We sing his glory, tell his worth.

Questions

1. What is the night sky like where you live? What can you see? How much can you recognise and identify?
2. Do you have any experiences of seeing the sky in a new way? What did they involve?

Exercises

1. Explore the sky above where you live. (A number of websites will help you to do this—for example, www.skymapper.co.uk and www.fourmilab.ch/yoursky.) How much of what you see did you already know? What surprised you?
2. Find a passage of the Bible that relates humankind to the heavens.
3. Find a map of the Holy Land at the time of Jesus' birth. Acquaint yourself with some of the journeys that would have been made as part of the birth narratives in the Gospels—from Nazareth to Jerusalem; from Jerusalem to Bethlehem; from the east 'to the place where the child was'.

Prayer

O God,
who by the leading of a star
manifested your only Son to the peoples of the earth:
mercifully grant that we,
who know you now by faith,
may at last behold your glory face to face;
through Jesus Christ your Son our Lord,
who is alive and reigns with you,
in the unity of the Holy Spirit,
one God, now and for ever.

COLLECT FOR EPIPHANY FROM *COMMON WORSHIP*

Never stop because you are afraid—you are never so likely to be wrong. Never keep a line of retreat: it is a wretched invention. The difficult is what takes a little time; the impossible is what takes a little longer.

NORWEGIAN EXPLORER FRIDTJOF NANSEN (1861–1930)

Into Your Hands

Encountering the touch of God

If you have enjoyed reading *Five Impossible Things to Believe Before Christmas*, you may be interested to know that Kevin Scully has also written *Into Your Hands* for BRF.

Beginning with the act of creation and moving on to reflect on the person and work of Jesus, this book considers how God—Father, Son, Spirit—has worked and continues to work to shape the events of human history. It also considers how we, as individuals, communities and churches, might respond. In a concluding section focusing on the events of Jesus' death and resurrection, we see his broken hands outstretched to bring healing and salvation as the mystery of redemption unfolds.

Each chapter concludes with questions for discussion or individual reflection, meditative exercises and a prayer. The book is also ideal material for reading and study during Lent.

As a 'taster' of *Into Your Hands*, the following pages reprint the book's Introduction and first chapter.

ISBN 978 1 84101 587 3   £5.99
Available from your local Christian bookshop or, in case of difficulty, direct from BRF using the order form on page 95.

Introduction

The hand of God

The ceiling of the Sistine Chapel in the Vatican has one of the world's most arresting creative images. It is also perhaps one of the best-known because it dares to combine its subject with its means of execution. Creativity is used to imagine creation in the world. We start by staring up at this ceiling but end up being taken somewhere else: Michelangelo's image provides us with a fundamental link between God and humanity. The artist has portrayed the hand of God stretching out to the hand of the first human.

The image on the front cover of this book is a section of a much larger scene. The artist chose to use what many might consider an unhelpful image of an old man with a beard, more Old Father Time than the Almighty, to portray the Creator God. By looking at the hands alone, we can concentrate our thoughts on the thrust of the creation story: 'Then the Lord God formed man from the dust of the ground, and breathed into his nostrils the breath of life; and the man became a living being' (Genesis 2:7).

In the section of the picture, the finger of God is just about to touch the finger of Adam. And that touch brings no less than life into the fleshly form. That touch can be seen as the loving exchange between Creator and the created. The touch is made on the tip of a finger, the outstretched extremity of a hand.

It is no accident that the artist concentrates on the hands of both God and man. On a relatively simple level, this might be understood in the complexity of human anatomy. The hand is one of the parts of the body that distinguish *homo sapiens* from other animals. Higher primates, such as apes and chimpanzees, have the ability to grasp with both hands and feet. The structure of these parts of their anatomy is different in humans. Because of this, it can be claimed that humans are the only beings that have true hands. There are 27 bones, overlaid by a network of muscles, tendons, tissues and blood vessels all hidden from the naked eye (another complex accumulation of working cells) by skin.

It is, however, more than the intricacy of human mechanics, wonderful as they are, that is of importance. After all, the hand of God is a potentially powerful metaphor, one that can lead to sustained meditation. Of course, we do not know what God's hands would have looked like in this encounter. Many would argue that to suggest God's hands have a human form, despite God's making humans in his own image, is unhelpful. That does not mean we draw back from using the metaphor. It can be used to solemn or comic effect. The footballer Diego Maradona termed his controversial goal from a handball in the quarter-final World Cup match between England and Argentina in 1986 as 'the hand of God'. Not surprisingly, his interpretation of this event was not universally accepted.

Yet the image of the hand of God meeting humanity remains an extraordinary encounter. Michelangelo provides us with a profound theological insight in visual form. He is showing a mutuality that will become lost. The images on the chapel ceiling trace this initial reaching out from God to man to the expulsion of Adam and Eve from the garden of seeming perfection. This is a vision of what the Church calls the Fall: transgression after temptation that leads to banishment. Put simply, it is a story of creative grace being usurped. In the beginning, however, there are both a hierarchy and a potential for equality.

The hierarchy is seen in the portrayal of God, surrounded by angels in the heavenly realm, about to touch the earthbound man. It is what might be considered the distance between the eternal and the temporal. The equality is in the act of creation itself. The hand of God reaches across the chasm and gives life to humanity. In doing so, life in our hands can become Godly. This is in keeping with how the Orthodox Church seeks to explain the actions of God in Jesus:

the divine became human so that humanity could become divine. It needs to be stressed that this is not based on human effort. Once again, it is the action of the Godhead that allows it.

At the point of creation there is no frustration or usurpation of that potential mutuality. That is captured in the visual wonder of the chapel, as well as in the verbal constructs of the Bible. The artist has provided a series of pictures that relate the narrative from the enlivening touch of God to a human to the expulsion from the garden of Eden.

We see what might have been—our intended destiny—when we look at the detail of Hand meeting hand. One gives to allow the other growth: the recipient reaches out to connect with the gift. Growth could find its terminus in that which led to its existence. That is the potential of creation. Much intellectual effort has been expended on trying to understand or display this potential. Yet a seemingly simple image—illusory simplicity, given the mastery of form and technique on Michelangelo's part—can encapsulate much of it.

The artist, for all the florid depiction of the creative genius of God, provides us with an image of a simple link. In this visual imagining we see established the theme that runs through so many of the early stories of the book of Genesis: God and humanity are linked. Creation is an act of consecration, never more strongly seen than in the life-giving touch of the Almighty. In this benediction we see what we are told in the first chapter of the opening book of the Bible: 'God saw everything that he had made, and indeed, it was very good' (Genesis 1:31).

This is more than some smug satisfaction on behalf of the moulder of the universe. In pronouncing it good, God has blessed the created order and thereby deemed it worthy of care. In this order we find that respect and honour are owed to creation. It may well be that, throughout Christian history, too much emphasis has been allowed to be placed on the separation between God and his creatures, captured in the doctrine of original sin, yet even that can be seen creatively. After all, we have the intellectual and imaginative gifts to deal with this and many other challenges. Such gifts can be used to good effect here. Having taken the future into their own hands, men and women lost touch with God. Much of the Bible—certainly the New Testament—concerns that separation and how it was overcome in and by Jesus.

That is a key to the Christian faith: God's hands took real human form... It is inevitable, then, that in talking of the hand of God we will also focus on Jesus. We will consider aspects of the life of Jesus, particularly his passion and death. We will especially focus on his hands and our potential to reflect the loving responsibility of faith.

There is a good reason for this focus. The highlight of the Christian liturgical year is Holy Week. Many parts of the Church embark on a special journey of events and services that commemorate the last days of Jesus in Jerusalem. It can be a busy time for priests and people alike. So much of the faith depends on what occurs in a relatively short period. Large parts of the Gospels are given over to the passion: the betrayal, suffering and death of Jesus. Such a concentration can bring many rewards and insights.

Each of the Holy Week celebrations or services has its roots in what happened to Jesus. These events begin with the riding of the donkey into the holy city, with Jesus being greeted and applauded by people who tear palms from trees and lay down their clothes in front of the animal. The rest of the week can be given to more restrained activities. These can take many forms: special services, *agape* meals, a gathering based on the *seder* meal of the Jewish Passover, marches of witness, walking the Stations of the Cross (14 tableaux that capture the journey from Pilate's judgment to the death of Jesus on the cross and his being laid in the tomb). To that end, some of the chapters in the latter part of this book will be given over to aspects of the interplay between the hands of Jesus and his followers.

In this book the emphasis will be on the creative interchange that flows from what is a relatively small canvas, captured in one of the images of Michelangelo's expanse of ceiling: the depiction of hands. We will find connections with the Bible and with our own lives. To aid this process of making connections, there are questions and exercises that readers may want to put to themselves or discuss in a group. Each chapter concludes with a prayer.

The exchange first seen in creation is the pattern of existence: God's hand stretching out to us, and ours reaching back to God. It is the pattern of the worshipping life. Once aware of the grace of God, we seek to praise the One who blesses us in our very being. This is caught in one of the songs of Israel:

Come, bless the Lord, all you servants of the Lord,
who stand by night in the house of the Lord!
Lift up your hands to the holy place,
and bless the Lord.
May the Lord, maker of heaven and earth,
bless you from Zion. (Psalm 134)

In this we can see that all human life is touched by the hand of God. If we sense God's touch, then we can reach out towards him in meditation and prayer. It is my hope that this book will provide its readers with an opportunity to do just that, to lift hands in prayer and strive to reconnect with the outstretched, loving hand of God.

God's hands are stretched out in life and in the death of Jesus on the cross. Our hands have a faithful demand on them to respond. Sometimes that responsibility can feel overwhelming. The stretching out of hands is, in many ways, a small journey but it can point to a longer journey. Thus we will be taking a journey that repeatedly returns to the loving gesture captured in the Sistine Chapel, a gesture in which God gives life to us all.

Chapter 1

_____   _____

And he brought them to see what he would call them

The Bible is full of surprises but many of them can seem hidden even to regular readers. Familiarity with some parts of scripture may allow us to overlook some interesting quirks. There is one such exciting development in the second chapter of Genesis. In that version of the creation narrative, God effectively hands over the world he has made into the care of the first man. There is imaginative power in this act.

Think of a child playing with toys in a sandpit. The child's hands have moved the sand around, sculpting an environment for the toy people that are to inhabit this new world. The hands, giant-like in comparison with the tiny figures in the new landscape, place each of the figures in its allotted spot. Then the child draws back and surveys the scene. The action of withdrawal gives life to the new world. She may initiate conversations, speaking on behalf of each player in her creative drama, but she imbues each doll with a personality of its own. She is part of her own making that includes a vast distance from the mind of the creator to the action of her new world.

It is possible to discern a similar quality of play in the second creation story in Genesis. The Almighty has wrought wonders: the man has been made; the breath of life has been blown into his nostrils; a garden has been planted; knowledge of good and evil has been placed in the midst of it all; rivers flow; precious metals and jewels are embedded. Then God places man in the middle of the garden.

Then the Lord God said, 'It is not good that the man should be alone; I will make him a helper as his partner.' So out of the ground the Lord God formed every animal of the field and every bird of the air, and brought them to the man to see what he would call them; and whatever the man called each living creature, that was its name. (Genesis 2:18–19)

This is arguably the place in scripture where God hands over the created order into the stewardship of humanity. In the earlier chapter of Genesis, one that tells a different version of the creation narrative, we have been assured that God looked on all that he had made and it was very good. In the second account there is a mighty difference: God pronounces a flaw. God himself announces that there is part of his work that is not good: the created being needs a helper.

In what follows, man seeks his helpmeet. In doing so, he is given both the care and charge of all that has been made for him. God places before the man each living creature that he has formed out of ground and watches to see what the man will name them. This is a poetic variation on the charge given to the woman and man, created on the same day, destined to be equal and blessed: 'God blessed them, and God said to them, "Be fruitful and multiply, and fill the earth and subdue it; and have dominion over the fish of the sea and over the birds of the air and over every living thing that moves upon the earth"' (Genesis 1:28).

Both creation stories point to the same core message: the world has been given into the care of humanity. From this follows a host of considerations. What is the difference between dominion and domination? Does responsibility to care for other species come only because humanity is more powerful? Is it proper to prey on them, even destroy them? Is protection of the weaker beings part of the onus of dominion? What is the proper management of a world where other creatures are there expressly for the sustenance of humanity?

There are many different responses to these questions and we might not agree over our answers. Indeed, we may find ourselves arguing for seemingly irreconcilable points of view. I have witnessed such debates and it can befuddle the listener to hear the combatants appealing to the same sources, some of them biblical, to support their contradictory arguments.

The key to these complexities for believers lies in a basic premise. God has given the world into our hands. We need to try to place ourselves at some distance to comprehend the effects of our actions. We have to challenge ourselves to think outside of the world in which we live in order to understand it better. In effect, this is trying to put ourselves into an impossible viewpoint, that of God. Mystics and poets can help us here. The song 'From a distance', penned by Julie Gold but popularised by Bette Midler, provides a perspective on the earth that may not be apparent as we live and work on it. Colours, shapes, even individual and societal relationships, can be understood in a new way when we realize that God watches us 'from a distance'...

A 14th-century mystic, Julian of Norwich, provides a useful image for us. In much the same way as we can compare the playing child to the distant God, we can look down on the world, seeing it in a hazelnut. In her *Revelations of Divine Love*, Julian wrote in perhaps her best known passage:

I saw that he is everything that we know to be good and helpful. In his love he clothes us, enfolds and embraces us; that tender love completely surrounds us, never to leave us. As I saw it he is everything that is good.

And he showed me more, a little thing, the size of a hazelnut, on the palm of my hand, round like a ball. I looked at it thoughtfully and wondered, 'What is this?' And the answer came, 'It is all that is made.' I marvelled that it continued to exist and did not suddenly disintegrate; it was so small. And again my mind supplied the answer, 'It exists, both now and forever, because God loves it.' In short, everything owes its existence to the love of God.

In this 'little thing' I saw three truths. The first is that God made it; the second is that God loves it; and the third is that God sustains it. But what he is who is in truth Maker, Keeper, and Lover I cannot tell; for until I am essentially united with him I can never have full rest or real happiness; in other words, until I am so joined to him that there is absolutely nothing between my God and me.

TRANS. CLIFTON WOLTERS (PENGUIN, 1966)

Let us stick with the idea of the world in our hands. Of course, Julian is trying to portray an image of how God might look at his creation. It is useful that the hazelnut is pictured as being in a hand, as the hand has substantial power. The nut is removed from view by simply by making a fist around it. It can be thrown away. Or it can be brought closer to the eye of the beholder.

Julian's passage is one of reassurance and tenderness. God loves his creation and the mystic's message is that it is tenderly held in God's hand. If we think of ourselves as holding this hazelnut, being the one in authority, like the child in the sandpit mentioned earlier, we can understand the responsibility of stewardship. Having been given dominion over the earth, it is incumbent that stewardship is carried out responsibly.

Some of this responsibility lies in the nature of that over which dominion has been given. A hazelnut is fairly hardy, with an armour-like shell. Anyone who has misguidedly attempted to crack one between their teeth will know that this is not an effective method. A sturdy nutcracker or even a hammer swung on to the nutshell on a hard surface is the least force required. The kernel can be ground for culinary purposes and is used in many foods, especially sweets. It is a central ingredient of praline in some kinds of chocolate and forms the basis of the Austrian *torte*, a multi-layered cake, the ground nuts being used as an alternative to flour.

Because of its hardiness a hazelnut is a particularly apt metaphor for the world. The natural order was, for centuries, considered resilient. Humanity could make incursions into it but, if left alone, it would begin a process of recovery. Nature seemed good at renewing itself. Even major disruptions—the devastation of Flanders' fields in the First World War being one major example—could be accommodated by the earth. If left alone, it can and does begin a process of rejuvenation.

Human endeavour has imperilled that aspect of the world. The impact of human activity on the natural order is now seen as significantly and permanently damaging and this presents us with a conundrum. If creation is an ongoing matter, and many would argue that it is, then creativity has a destructive side. Each 'advance' in modern living comes at some cost.

This reflects a deep theological and natural truth. Having been given dominion over the world, humanity acts in a seemingly God-like manner: it can build up or destroy. Much of the natural order cannot compete with the effects of sustained interference. The stewardship of natural resources requires thought, effort and management. Every human action has some aftershock, even if minimal. A walk on the grass leaves imprints, a trail of minor damage. If this is random and unsustained, there is no problem. But if a route is repeatedly used, a path soon forms and the grass dies. At first this can be helpful. Those who walk in the country can discern the right of way by the path, yet it can lead to erosion, especially on popular routes. Water will channel along the path, making it deeper, and another path is made on firmer ground to one side.

The very fact of our being alive can be instructive in understanding our impact on the world. Our breath changes the make-up of the atmosphere. Too many people breathing the same air in a confined space can lead to stuffiness, a lack of oxygen and, ultimately, suffocation.

We are more familiar with considering the impact of the motor car on the environment. Land is absorbed in the building of roads. Habitats are eradicated. Species are reduced or even made extinct. The air quality in the proximity of roads degenerates. A build-up of traffic uses more fuel, thus depleting global stocks of petroleum. How many people think of this impact when they get into the car to pop down to the shops, to collect the children from school or to go to church?

Many church leaders speak of the need to care for God's creation but this does not seem to stop building schemes that require large amounts of electricity and other resources to support the latest initiative. Many new church buildings draw on fashions in other parts of the construction industry. How many church committees try to quantify the ongoing impact of a new building in terms of its electricity consumption? Is the heating of the church building efficient? Are there methods that can minimise the overall effect on natural resources?

In some congregations success is measured by the size of the car park and how quickly it fills before a service. What would happen if such churches promoted alternative transport: walking, cycling, car pooling or public transport? Are smaller, local gatherings potentially more beneficial to a greater good?

Some churches generate a new service book for every gathering. What is the cost of this in electricity? What happens to the booklets after their use? Are they thrown away or recycled? Similar questions can be asked about provision of refreshments. Are they served in reusable or in disposable cups? Has any discussion been had over where the tea or coffee comes from? Are the producers paid a fair price for their goods?

There are personal, social and political implications in the very fact of being, and the story of creation links us to them through God. People of faith need to think through these implications. They are not easy. We cannot bluff our way past them with pat answers. Dealing with them takes thought, consideration and reflection and, for people of faith, it requires prayer.

The actions of humanity lead to many consequences for the natural world. Creation has been placed into our hands. What we do with it matters.

Prayer

Creator God,
you hold us and the rest of your making in your hand.
Your love for us dares to give into our hands
that which you have made.
Help us to consider the impact we have on your world.
Challenge us to look beyond our immediate needs
to see how we might fit into the web of your gift of life.
We ask this through your revealed self,
Jesus, in the sustaining life of the Spirit.
Amen

ORDERFORM

REF	TITLE					PRICE	QTY	TOTAL
587 3	Into Your Hands					£5.99		

POSTAGE AND PACKING CHARGES					Postage and packing	
Order value	UK	Europe	Surface	Air Mail	Donation	
£7.00 & under	£1.25	£3.00	£3.50	£5.50	**TOTAL**	
£7.10–£30.00	£2.25	£5.50	£6.50	£10.00		
Over £30.00	FREE	prices on request				

Name _____ Account Number _____

Address _____

_____ Postcode _____

Telephone Number_____

Email _____

Payment by: ❑ Cheque ❑ Mastercard ❑ Visa ❑ Postal Order ❑ Maestro

Card no ❑❑❑❑ ❑❑❑❑ ❑❑❑❑ ❑❑❑❑ ❑❑❑

Valid from ❑❑❑❑ Expires ❑❑❑❑ Issue no. ❑❑❑

Security code* ❑❑❑ *Last 3 digits on the reverse of the card.
ESSENTIAL IN ORDER TO PROCESS YOUR ORDER

Shaded boxes for Maestro use only

Signature _____ Date _____

All orders must be accompanied by the appropriate payment.

Please send your completed order form to:
BRF, 15 The Chambers, Vineyard, Abingdon OX14 3FE
Tel. 01865 319700 / Fax. 01865 319701 Email: enquiries@brf.org.uk

❑ Please send me further information about BRF publications.

Available from your local Christian bookshop.   BRF is a Registered Charity

brf

Resourcing your spiritual journey

through...

- Bible reading notes
- Books for Advent & Lent
- Books for Bible study and prayer
- Books to resource those working with under 11s in school, church and at home

- Quiet days and retreats
- Training for primary teachers and children's leaders
- Godly Play
- Barnabas RE Days

For more information, visit the **brf** website at **www.brf.org.uk**